Mark Johnston addresses a su  f
historic evangelicalism befor
liberal ecumenism of the W   s
increasingly failed to create a desired hierarchical unity,
evangelicals have sadly overreacted and lost marvellous
opportunities for grassroots expressions of the true unity they
share in the gospel. Johnston points the way forward, by tackling
the biblical and practical issues head on, and by urging us to
think more soberly about John 17. This is a sagacious and
practical little book.

Dr. John H. Armstrong
President
Reformation & Revival Ministries

With warmth and sanity, Mark Johnston steers us on an
eminently Biblical path through the principles and practicalities
of pursuing the desire of Jesus Christ for his people to be one.
This book should prove a rebuke to the hard-hearted, a corrective
to the soft-headed, and a stimulus to all evangelicals of good
will towards God-honouring unity.

John Benton,
editor *Evangelicals Now*

Never, in all its long and often courageous history, has the
evangelical community in Britain been so aggressively
fragmented as it is today. The course and causes are often
complex, mostly tragic, and the cure has seemed intractable.
Either we progressively narrow the basis of unity until few quite
fit our small circle, or we throw it so wide that no one is excluded,
however bizarre or unorthodox their views. Mark Johnston adds
not just another book on unity, but offers a strong biblical
framework for it – including the model of the tri-unity in the
Godhead, the work of the Holy Spirit in the life of the church,
and the priority of unity exampled in the prayers of Jesus Christ.

No Christian can read this book without being convinced that something must be done to create harmony in the local church and unity between evangelical congregations. The challenge when you have finished reading is to find those ways of doing it.

Brian H. Edwards

You in Your Small Corner

The Elusive Dream of Evangelical Unity

Mark G. Johnston

Christian Focus

© Mark Johnston
ISBN 1 85792 381 2

Published in 1999
by
Christian Focus Publications,
Geanies House, Fearn, Ross-shire,
IV20 1TW, Great Britain.

Cover design by Owen Daily

Contents

To
Mum and Dad
Models and Mentors in a Multitude of Ways

Preface

For anyone to venture into the treacherous waters of a discussion of Christian unity is surely to have their sanity called into question! It is something akin to wading into a swamp, or wandering into a minefield. There can be few issues in the Christian church which have provoked as much strife as the need 'to preserve the unity of the Spirit in the bond of peace' (Eph. 4:3). Why then venture into print?

The simple answer is because the Bible attaches far more importance to the unity of the church than the church has often acknowledged. Paul uses the strongest possible language when he says to a disunited church in Ephesus, '*Spare no effort* to preserve the unity of the Spirit in the bond of peace' (Eph. 4:3, *my translation*). If truth be told, Christians have spared themselves a great deal of effort in this particular area of their faith. It has been one of the most fraught areas of church life. Even in the smallest unit of the local congregation, genuine unity can be hard to find. When we come to expressing anything that resembles it across denominational, cultural and theological divides it seems at times to be impossible. The way to handle that has been either to try to rationalize the texts of Scripture which speak to the subject and make them mean something we feel we can cope with, or else to just ignore them.

It has been a personal obsession of mine for many years that we simply cannot afford the luxury of either of these options because if we do, we are being untrue to our Lord and Saviour who alone is King and Head of his church. I

suspect there has been a hint of the divine sense of humour
in the way that God in his providence has ordered the course
of my own life in such a way as to foster that obsession. A
humour which first struck me one evening when I was
introduced at a meeting as 'a hybrid: born an Anglican,
became a Presbyterian and about to marry a Baptist!' (As
if to leave no stone of ecclesiastical polity unturned, the
hybrid is currently the minister of an Independent Reformed
Church in London!) Although my personal convictions are
Reformed and Presbyterian (and are wholeheartedly shared
by my dear wife) it has amazed me how much liberty they
still give to move in wider church circles and enjoy rich
fellowship with the broader family of God.

It is little short of tragic to see the way a theological and
denominational ghetto-mentality can rob God's people of
a depth of joy and degree of usefulness in God's work which
can only be found in a wider relationship with his people
wherever they are found. Only when we have the courage
to cross some of these boundaries – within the limits of
biblical integrity – do we find that new horizons open up
for us which take us closer to the heart of God's purpose in
redemption.

It would be pretentious to think that any of the
components in my 'hybrid' experience either qualify or
entitle me to write on the subject of evangelical unity, but
I hope they provide something of an apology for this book.
What follows is nothing more than the clumsy and
imperfect reflections of a pilgrim looking back on the short
road by which he has come thus far. I hope they convey
something of the beauty of that biblical variegated oneness
of the church – a beauty which is entirely the work of our
God and Saviour. I hope too that they highlight the way

that we are all involved in enriching and shaping each other in the wider church to which we belong in fellowship with Christ.

I am indebted to numerous people along the way for shaping my own thoughts in this complex and controversial field. To my father, who is also the minister of the Episcopal church in which I grew up, I am ever grateful for that spirit of evangelical catholicity he displayed by inviting men to preach in his church, not on the basis of a denominational tag, but on whether or not they were faithful to God's Word. To my theological *alma mater* – Westminster Seminary in Philadelphia – where students from many ecclesiastical backgrounds all over the world came together in an arena of robust, yet loving interaction to our mutual edification. To my brothers and sisters in the Evangelical Presbyterian Church in Ireland for allowing me to be involved with their inter-church relations work through the *British Evangelical Council* and the *International Conference of Reformed Churches*. Finally to my brothers and sisters in my present congregation of Grove Chapel in South London, who, despite their independent polity, see that the church of Christ is bigger than any local congregation and acknowledge that in practice through true and meaningful fellowship with other churches.

All quotations from the Bible cited in this book are taken from the *New American Standard Bible (Updated Edition)*, unless otherwise indicated.

Grove Chapel
Camberwell
January 1999

Introduction

'The denominations are in meltdown. By the early part of the new millennium, the ecclesiastical map of Great Britain will be barely recognizable!' So said a prominent evangelical minister of the Church of England at a recent consultation of church leaders in Britain. He was not trying to be unduly alarmist by this comment, simply attempting to make a realistic observation about the church scene in general as the turn of a millennium draws near.

His observations are not isolated. Towards the end of the 1980s Hans Kung, speaking at an ecumenical gathering in Belfast, Northern Ireland, made similar remarks. As he surveyed some two thousand years of church history, he identified five major epochs of church life, each dominated by particular traits and emphases and punctuated by distinct periods of flux. These intervening periods he saw as times of struggle between conflicting theologies, but which settled into new periods of fresh direction for Christendom in general, each coloured by a dominant theology and practice. The bottom line of his analysis was his saying that the church world-wide at the end of the twentieth century finds itself in such a time of flux. Both the Roman Catholic Church and the historic Protestant churches, in the western world at least, are experiencing significant internal upheavals and are struggling to relate to an increasingly post-Christian world. The future, according to Kung, lies in the ability of the Pentecostal/Charismatic axis to bridge the divide between these major church groupings and lead them into a new era of theology and practice, suited for the twenty-first century.

Whatever the correct appraisal of the current scene may be, there can be no doubt that we are living in times of ecclesiastical and theological change and it would be naïve not to see the need to respond. The fragmentation which has become a feature of life in general is increasingly invading every quarter of church life, leaving few Christians unaffected. This raises the question of how we are to respond in a biblical and constructive way which does not compromise the truth which lies at the heart of the Christian faith.

The starting point must surely be that we face the present situation honestly and realistically. The words of the children's hymn, 'You in your small corner and I in mine', depict all too well the naïve approach to church life that prevails among many Christians. They have such a blinkered view of reality that, so long as things seem well in their own little ecclesiastical world denominationally, or their own special interest group congregationally, they are content. In adopting such an outlook, however, they manage to cut themselves off from a wider fellowship in the true church for which they are both responsible and accountable. The men of the Westminster Assembly well expressed what Scripture says about the nature of the professing church of Christ when they said, 'The purest churches under heaven are subject both to mixture and error.'[1] Put bluntly, there is no such thing as a perfect church. God's people on this side of glory must be prepared to live with the tension and frustration of things never being as they ought to be in God's family.

Acknowledging that, however, does not open the door for complacency. The goal of a family united in and around the truth, at every level of our life together, is ever set before us by the God who presides over his family. The consequence of that is the longing for such unity which stirs in the heart of every true child of his. In the same way that even the most divided of natural families still retain some kind of instinct for its family identity, so in God's spiritual family the same is true.

There are numerous complexities which intrude upon any consideration of this issue. Most obviously there is the question of the levels of church life upon which unity must impinge. When the Scriptures speak about the oneness of the people of God there is what seems to be a deliberate ambiguity as to where it must be manifest. At the most basic level there is the need for unity within the local congregation. Every church has suffered the pain of friction and tension within its membership and not a few have suffered the anguish of schism. The horizons of fellowship, however, are broader than the local church. That raises the question, then, of how churches in a particular locality relate to one another and even that question is not straightforward! It is one thing to relate to other local churches within a defined denominational grouping, quite another to relate to those who belong to a different group. There is a street in Belfast with the illustrious name of 'Templemore Avenue' where, at one time, there were said to be eleven evangelical churches in one square mile, yet none of them would have anything to do with the others. The average pagan might find that a little hard to understand.

Of course the ecclesiastical maze doesn't stop there. Is there not a place for asking how churches are to relate at wider levels – regionally, nationally and even internationally? It is possible (and it has been practice) to pursue links like this in various ways. Some churches have developed such links through denominational groupings, others have taken an inter-denominational approach (with strict rules about relationships and the degree of fellowship which may be enjoyed). This invariably leads to a level of ecclesiastical bureaucracy which rivals any local government and threatens many rain-forests in Brazil. A simpler and more pragmatic approach has often been to take the non-denominational route with minimal requirements for precise doctrinal agreement. This expresses itself in the many para-church organizations and co-operative ventures in which Christians happily involve themselves, but which often raise hard questions about respecting the beliefs and practices of the parties involved.

As if these concerns were not enough to trouble us, the road to unity among the people of God is littered with the debris of the schisms of the past, the wounds and bruises that lead to fear and suspicion about the present, and the greatest variable of them all: the personal chemistry of the figures involved! On top of that, we have the legacy of almost one hundred years of liberal ecumenism through the *World Council of Churches* and its many regional expressions. This movement is rapidly heading beyond the confines of inter-church fellowship into the realms of inter-faith dialogue and co-operation. In the midst of it all the colossal shadow of the Roman Catholic Church has never been far away. The significance of that in recent years for conservative Protestant churches has taken an interesting turn with the emergence of *Evangelicals and Catholics Together* and the involvement of high-profile evangelical leaders.[2]

Besides all of these concerns, many others proffer

themselves as factors in the wider picture, many of them peculiar to the post-modern and post-Christian age in which we find ourselves. Pressure to tolerate and be tolerated is the inevitable consequence of a pluralistic outlook on the world and on religions. General reaction against clearly defined structures mitigates against an approach to unity which tries to operate within a clearly understood doctrine of the church. Debate over the meaning of meaning has fuelled an ever-increasing reaction against giving place to creeds and confessions in church life. Then, to top it all, there is the spirit of weariness and cynicism among those who have laboured for a lifetime to bring Christians and churches together and all apparently to no avail.

The waters of unity have never been so muddy, yet the need for genuine and meaningful unity has never been so great. The only one who can afford to be smug while the Kingdom of Light appears to fragment is the one who presides over the Kingdom of Darkness.

As we dare to address these enormous concerns there are many angles from which we could approach them. It is most tempting to take a purely pragmatic line and suggest how church unity might be given a higher profile. The danger there is that unity becomes an end in itself and the quest for it will become even more like an exercise in rainbow-chasing. Instead it would seem more constructive to place unity in the broader biblical context of the character of God and his eternal purpose in redemption. As with so many aspects of the Christian life, unity among God's people is not found through seeking unity, but rather seeking God. My aim, therefore, is to begin by recognizing the way in which the Bible sets the unity of God's family within the framework of the unity of the Godhead – a

significant element in what it means to bear the image of
God on earth; then go on to see the way in which Scripture
is our only reliable guide and provides the only workable
framework in the quest for unity; then finally consider the
practicalities which flow out of this foundation into the
actual relationships of the people of God.

My decision to address unity as 'evangelical' is quite
deliberate. Although it is an adjective which has been
grossly devalued in the religious currency of our day, it
still retains enough significance to remind us that true
Christianity must be biblical. It must be defined and shaped
– however imperfectly – by the *Evangel*, the Word of God.
Hence true fellowship between Christians must likewise
be defined and shaped by that same Word. It is possible to
speak about Christian unity, but that is a completely
vacuous term if it is divorced from the Bible that alone can
explain what 'Christian' means. Thus any attempt to pursue
unity in that vein amounts to nothing more than 'holding
hands in the dark'.

Any volume on the subject of unity will inevitably, at
least to some extent, be a child of its time. Its precise content
and shape will be affected by the issues of the day. This
volume is no exception. It has been born in an age when
deep and unsettling questions have been raised in
practically every quarter of the evangelical community. In
the United Kingdom, the long-standing rift between
evangelicals who have remained within theologically
mixed denominations and those who have seceded into free
evangelical groupings of one sort or another is once again
under scrutiny. A generation of Christians and church
leaders has emerged who know little of the issues which
caused that rift in the evangelical family in the first place.

The questions of where they belong and to whom they should relate are very much to the fore. In America the widespread erosion of historic evangelical theology and practice has led to such attempts at recovery of what is being lost as the *Cambridge Declaration*[3] and the formation of such groupings as the *Alliance of Confessing Evangelicals*.[4] The emergence of the Roman Catholic dimension in all of this has called into question the very understanding of historic Protestant Evangelicalism itself. All of these factors are current in discussions at this time and are affecting the course of history. Each in its own way will affect this book.

Chapter One

God's Multicoloured Wisdom
The Architect and Setting

One of the most disturbing and yet enriching experiences of my Christian life was to venture outside the evangelical sub-culture in which I had grown up. The Province of Ulster – Northern Ireland – is renowned for its conservative Christianity, and for those for whom this has been their only experience it can be deeply unsettling to step outside. Thus, when I set off for Philadelphia at the age of 21 to train for the ministry, I was not quite sure what to expect. Even though I was heading for a theological seminary which was well known for its conservatism, and even though I quickly attached myself to a church which was the closest equivalent to what I had left behind in Ireland, I have vivid memories of some three months or more of thinking these Americans had a very poor understanding of what it meant to be an evangelical. I found myself being critical of their piety and their practice in church life and feeling distinctly uncomfortable about many things. I even questioned whether or not I belonged among them.

The problem, of course, was that I was measuring what I saw and heard by the standard of what I had been used to at home and which I automatically assumed to be the norm. The reality which began to dawn on me was that the norm does not begin with us and our limited sphere of understanding and experience, but rather with God and with his Word.

A lecturer in another institution in Philadelphia used to tease his classes in the same series of lectures delivered each year by asking, 'How far is it to New York?' The answer which came back on almost every occasion was '120 miles' – the approximate distance between the two cities. Successive classes were perplexed to see him respond by shaking his head. Only one student apparently has ever answered the question correctly by saying, 'It depends on where you start!' That little exercise in relative geography powerfully illustrates the way that we instinctively regard ourselves as the centre of our little universe, an instinct which does not automatically disappear with conversion.

Being physically relocated in a very different evangelical sub-culture forced me to take seriously the centrality of God and his Word as the norm for all Christian experience and practice. That meant taking off the cultural blinkers which up until then had hindered my appreciation of the breadth and diversity within the true family of God.

It was brought home to me in a very graphic way listening to Sinclair Ferguson preach in Tenth Presbyterian Church, a large downtown congregation in Philadelphia. He had been expounding the verse in the third chapter of Ephesians which speaks of God's 'manifold wisdom' (Eph. 3:10) and the way in which it is put on display in the life of the church. The point he was making was that the unity within the diversity of the church is a wonderful reflection of the wisdom of God in salvation. Then, to press this point home, he paused and told the congregation of around a thousand people to look around them. There were people of every conceivable description in the gathering. There were wealthy people and street people, educated and illiterate, men and women, young and old, black, white and coloured – the permutations were numerous. 'There you see it,' he said. 'We have in this building what men have dreamed of but have never managed to achieve by politics, force or hard labour; yet God has achieved it by his grace.'

The truth contained in that verse encapsulates the sheer wonder of what God has planned, has accomplished and is accomplishing in the salvation of his people. It is there we must begin if we are going to understand the basis of the unity we should enjoy in his church.

It would be possible for us to go to quite a range of Scriptures which address God's plan for unity among his people, many of which have been well explored in other books on this subject. However, I think it will be helpful for us to consider one verse which has not featured very prominently in the discussion, yet which is undoubtedly central to the issue. It is the verse to which we have already alluded in the sermon preached that night in Philadelphia. If we take the perspective that the one, united church of Jesus Christ is like a building (1 Pet. 2:5), then it follows there must be an architect and master-builder who lies behind this spiritual edifice – and that can only be God. Behind the elaborate design of the end-product there lies the intricate wisdom of the great Designer. It is to this divine wisdom that Paul directs his Ephesian audience. Let us pore over the 'drawings' for a moment to appreciate something of the problem facing the architect and what lies behind the solution he proposes.

An Earthly Problem

Every architect coming on site faces a problem of one sort or another. The main problem is how to get a new building in place where currently there is either none at all, or one which is imperfect. The former scenario is always less of a problem because he is starting from scratch, the latter more of a problem because he must work within the confines of the existing structure and space. The plans he comes up with must take account of the needs of the situation with which he is faced.

Thus as the divine architect comes 'on site' in the world, he is confronted by a problem: that of a fallen, fragmented race. Sin has not only affected the upward dimension of man's relationship with God in heaven, but also the horizontal dimension of the relationship between human beings on earth. The broken fellowship with God which was the major consequence of the fall (Gen. 3:22-24) is very quickly followed by the broken fellowship of the human family (Gen. 4:1-8). The story of the human race ever since that point of history has been one of ever-increasing fragmentation in families, communities, nations and the world. The problem we face as human beings is the same as confronts God: how can this process be reversed? It is true that God faces the problem from an altogether different perspective, as we shall see below, but its essence is the same: sin has divided humanity and somehow its unity needs to be restored.

The issue for Paul as he writes to the church in Ephesus is the fact that this earthly problem – the product of a fallen world – has reared its ugly head in the church. The age-old division between Jew and Gentile, loaded as it was with intense nationalistic and religious feeling, was having a devastating effect on the unity of God's people in that region. (We do not have to read far in the New Testament to realize that this was *the* issue which more than any other preoccupied the emerging church of that time.) At one level it was an issue of national identity and pride. The Jewish people had a fervent consciousness of their history, a passion which had been galvanized by years of oppression, persecution and deportation. Even when they were scattered to the four corners of the earth these people carried with them a profound desire to retain their distinct identity. This inevitably affected the way they viewed the peoples of surrounding nations. Their sense of identity was significantly reinforced by the way their national roots were closely intertwined with religious roots in God's unusual dealings with that nation as recorded in the Old Testament. The regulations God had given his people in his Law had much to say about their relationships with the non-Jewish (Gentile) nations around them. Although these rules were clear and had their purpose, the most zealous Jews over the centuries had added to God's laws in this area, widening the gap even further between these peoples.

As Paul preached the gospel of Jesus Christ to Gentiles as well as Jews and saw many from both sides of that divide converted, he very quickly discovered that old prejudice died hard. Many converted Jews were insisting that the cultural trappings of their former religious system – rooted as it was in Old Testament revelation – were to be required of those from a Gentile background who came into the church. Thus issues like circumcision, holy days and ceremonial practices were being pressed upon new Christians who found them quite alien to the way they understood the gospel. The problem reached such a pitch that it required a special international assembly of church leaders to convene in Jerusalem specifically to debate the issue (Acts 15:1-35).

The bottom line (as concluded by the Jerusalem council) was that these Jewish believers had unjustifiable views about their own cultural background and they were not entitled to insist upon these details in their relationships with Gentile converts. They were bringing the problems of a fallen world into the altogether different sphere of the life of the church.

Although the Jew–Gentile controversy is no longer a burning issue in church life today (though it is far from extinct), it well illustrates the kind of problem that is commonplace in many quarters of church life and fellowship. The old sinful prejudices of a fallen world are imported into the redeemed community of the people of God. It has manifest itself in some situations through racial prejudice – the make-up of a church being determined along ethnic lines. In others the prejudice is sectarian, or social, intellectual, or even theological. The sinful barriers which have divided the secular community have simply continued (and in some cases been reinforced) in the spiritual community. Where that is the case, something is seriously wrong and it calls into question the credibility of the gospel itself.

A Heavenly Perspective

The most serious aspect of this earthly problem was quite simply that humanly speaking it had and has no solution. It is possible to engage in political negotiation between divided communities – as seen in the much-fêted 'peace processes' of recent times – and come up with paper settlements which can be policed and enforced and yet never succeed in changing stubborn human hearts. Thus the fragile peace of these communities is always only one incitement away from disintegration. Beneath the surface issues of the particular problems that divide people is the deeper problem of hearts which are in the grip of sin with all its destructive powers.

It is this sombre reality which has gathered a fascinated, yet unseen, audience to observe the drama being played out in the arena of the world. Paul refers directly to them in this verse as 'the rulers and the authorities in the heavenly places'. By these he means not only the angels and heavenly beings who wait on God's command, but also the dark powers of evil who, although they are in perpetual rebellion against God, know better than any human being that God is in control (Eph. 6:12). These angels and demons, the invisible inhabitants of the cosmos, watch on as events unfold on earth to see where they will lead.

These unseen beings were there from the beginning as part of God's creation. They were very much aware of the uniqueness of man in God's creating purpose and conscious also of the drastic consequences when one of their number – Satan – seduced Adam and Eve into sharing his rebellion against God their Maker (Gen. 3:1-7). The pinnacle of God's creation – man, made in the image of God – was now under God's curse and personally incapable of undoing the damage done through his actions. From that point onwards his nature was fallen, sin was in his very being. As a creature it was, in the words of Augustine of Hippo, 'not possible for him not to sin'. The burning question in the heavenly realms thenceforth was, 'What can God do about it?'

God himself appeared to be in an insoluble dilemma: a dilemma which Paul is quick to point out when he speaks of God as being 'just and the justifier of the one who has faith in Jesus' (Rom. 3:26). God's problem is that of maintaining his own integrity. How can he remain consistent with his own justice and righteousness and yet accept unrighteous sinners? What kind of divine wisdom could be invoked to resolve this problem? The heavenly powers, Paul tells us, watch transfixed as the plan of God's redemption unfolds on the stage of human history. It soon becomes apparent to them that the divine wisdom which lies behind it is not bland and monochrome as is even the best of creaturely wisdom, rather it is 'manifold', or, more accurately, 'multicoloured'. As we shall see shortly, the wisdom of God which underlies the salvation of men transcends anything that could have been expected of him.

The reason these creatures of the unseen realm are so interested in God's concern for the human race is simply that the destiny of creation turns on the destiny of man. As the sin of man brought God's anathema upon the world and universe (Gen. 3:17-20), so his redemption marks their deliverance (Rom. 8:20-21). Those who belong to the real, but invisible, order of creation, then, have a vested interest in what happens to our race. God's grace towards the penitent through his Son is the guarantee of the promised renewal of all things (Matt. 19:28), whereas his judgement of the wicked will seal the fate of the angels who shared in Satan's rebellion and expulsion from heaven.

The implication of this seemingly insignificant and arguably irrelevant comment is enormous. If the issues which are played out in the life of the church have a bearing on the destiny of the cosmos, then it puts the affairs of the

church into an altogether different perspective. No longer
do we have the right to trivialize our differences within the
household of faith. No matter how much we may try to
internalize our problems within our own little congregation,
or our own little grouping – depriving outsiders of
incriminating information about our squabbles – our affairs
are on public and inter-cosmic display. To know that we
are being observed by a host of interested and affected
parties must surely affect how we conduct ourselves.

The issues of church unity stretch far beyond the limits
of local church life, or the horizons of denominational
distinctives. They take us into the outer reaches of the
universe itself.

An Eternal Plan

It should hardly surprise us, given the perspective Paul has
introduced, that these issues do not fall into the category
of some divine contingency plan, but rather are central to
God's eternal purpose – a fact that Paul states explicitly in
the next verse. Going back for a moment to the scale of the
dilemma facing the divine architect when he comes on site
in the world, we now realize that it is under control. God is
not faced with something that has taken him by surprise,
nor posed him with an insurmountable challenge. Rather,
it fell within the mystery of his wise and perfect plan.

Again this was to have a very practical impact upon the
problem in the church at Ephesus. For the Jewish and
Gentile parties caught up in the controversy, it was only
natural for them to view their situation from their own
perspective and perhaps even invoke God as being on their
side. God was saying quite simply that both sides were
wrong. To view the problem from the finite, fallen

perspective of either side of a human dispute was guaranteed to misunderstand the situation and fail to resolve it. The issues, by definition, could be seen only within the limits of space, time and human interest of that particular moment. Any understanding of them was bound to be distorted by reducing them to the level of human plan and purpose and the party spirit which entangles them.

God wisely and rightly elevates the matter to a different plane. He provides that eternal vantage point which transforms our reading of all history and every situation in life. Our life as God's creatures – individually and collectively – can be straightened out only when we are brought back into willing submission to God and his eternal purpose.

It is not hard to see how strife within the church and between churches is painfully and needlessly exacerbated when professing Christians refuse to see their situation from God's point of view. Indeed they defame God by daring to press him into their service rather than submitting themselves to his. It is of the very essence of sin to turn the universe around and make it man-centred and not God-centred, while it is of the essence of salvation to restore it to its proper axis.

An Unlikely Stage

We have all watched amusing scenes in cartoons in which the characters think they are doing something completely unobserved, then, to their surprise, a spotlight clicks on and they realize they are in the middle of a stage and the focus of attention. They blush with embarrassment and the action takes a different turn.

In a sense Paul turns the spotlight on the church in Ephesus in a way which must have brought not a few blushes to faces in that congregation. An issue which they really thought to be a private affair, tucked away in an unseen corner of the Christian world, was actually a most public affair exposed to the gaze of a watching world and a cosmic audience whom we have already noted.

The stage upon which God has chosen to exhibit his 'multicoloured wisdom' is none other than the church in the world. It is his chosen medium of communication. Without question it is a most unlikely stage, because it is so imperfect. Yet its very imperfection has a place in its being the display-board of God's wisdom. The lingering sinfulness of man which continues to contaminate the life of God's people leaves them with the instinct for boasting in self and personal achievement, and the desire to look more to self in salvation than to God and his wonderful provision. Thus Paul has had to make clear in the earlier ground-work of this epistle that salvation is all of grace, received simply with the open hand of faith, precisely so that there is no room for boasting and self-congratulation (Eph. 2:9-10). The ongoing presence of sin and failure in even the best of churches is a graphic reminder that none of us has earned our way into God's family and is a powerful declaration to the world that God does not operate on the basis of merit.

The implications of how the drama is played out are striking. It is one thing to pay lip-service to a doctrine of salvation by grace, as did the Ephesians and even the Pharisees; it is an altogether different thing to build it in to the warp and weft of Christian living. It is only as our faces are pressed into the dirty reality of our sinfulness and failure, even as Christians, that our hearts are truly captivated and enraptured by the power of saving grace. It becomes something which actually engages both mind and will in a conscious fashion, drawing us, as opposed to coercing us, back into a right relationship with God.

For God's people to see the church, not as their own little private arena and domain, but as God's centre-piece of history, brings a new dynamic into the relationships which unfold within that context. If we take seriously what Paul is saying, we will be impelled to plead with God for grace – for the daily filling of his Spirit (Eph. 5:18), which alone can provide the wherewithal to honour him and bless each other.

The Central Figure
Such concerns will of necessity drive us to Jesus. Hence Paul brings what he is saying into sharp focus with the comment, 'This was in accordance with the eternal purpose which He carried out in Christ Jesus our Lord' (Eph. 3:11). The central figure on the stage of the church will never be the kind of figure that is so often elevated to that position: gifted leader, eloquent preacher, charismatic personality, or whoever, rather God's own Son, the Lord Jesus Christ. The ramifications of Paul's statement run deep and wide.

They clearly take us to the cross as the place where the destiny of God's people was secured. It is through the cross uniquely that both Jew and Gentile are brought near to the God from whom sin has alienated them (Eph. 2:13-16). It was there on that hill outside Jerusalem that a decisive transaction took place in which the Son of God gave himself specifically and efficaciously for his people. He did not merely die to make salvation possible, but rather to secure and guarantee as reality the redemption of the entirety of God's elect. He died explicitly to 'save *His* people from their sins' (Matt. 1:21). The central place given to the Lord's Supper – the sacrament of the cross – in the life of the church is the perpetual reminder that she owes her existence to that event. There, supremely, the multicoloured nature of divine wisdom was revealed in that with one fell swoop divine justice was satisfied and the floodgates of divine love thrown open. The seemingly irreconcilable aspects of the character of God were reconciled:

Lovingkindness and truth have met together;
Righteousness and peace have kissed each other (Ps. 85:10).

There and there supremely the wisdom of God has eclipsed the wisdom of men and made perfect provision for our deepest needs.

Christ stands centre-stage in the life of the church in the forensic sense of what he accomplished as substitute for his people. In addition to this, however, he is the *source* of life for the church and all who truly belong within her fellowship. He is the true vine from whom all branches must draw their spiritual life and vitality. The church is never seen as a tedious organization, or a monochrome establishment, rather as a vibrant living organism. She is a body with a head (1 Cor. 12:27), a bride united to her husband (Eph. 5:32), a vine with its branches (John 15:5), an army animated by the Spirit of God (Ezek. 37:10). She lives only because she is joined to the risen, exalted Christ in living, vital union. Existentially she depends on him. Without him she can do nothing (John 15:5). Where he is absent from a church, there is only an empty shell of lives which have the form of godliness, but know nothing of its power (2 Tim. 3:5).

The reason which lies behind disintegration and fragmentation in all too many churches is to be found, sadly, at this critical level. Their exercises in pulling the church together are every bit as macabre as the efforts to manipulate the lifeless limbs of a corpse and no less futile in what they accomplish. A church that knows nothing of Jesus can know nothing of life. Before there can be genuine, visible evidence of life in a church, there must be the invisible reality of life in the hearts of its people.

Where there is that life from above, even in its faintest flickerings, its welfare is dependent upon actively looking to the Jesus through whom the church lives. He must be consciously given his place in the heart of church life if the church is to derive practical benefit from him. As he is the focal point of the worship of the church in heaven (Rev. 5:11-14), so he must be the focus of the worship of the church on earth. In song, through prayer, by the Word read and preached, through the sacraments, in the fellowship, in church politics and business, in everything and every way he must be given pre-eminence, because he alone holds the key to blessing.

The Master Plan of the Master Planner

It is one thing to look at a building and even to wander through its corridors and admire its rooms. It is another thing to have its architect spread his plans on the table and explain detail and design which are not apparent to a casual observer and yet which are critical to the stability and structure of the edifice. To see the plan that lies behind the product opens wider the doors of appreciation and usefulness to all who use the building.

So, to an even greater extent, with the church. Written

off in the minds of many, not just in an unbelieving world, but even in an all-too-cynical church, nevertheless the plan of God throws light and dignity upon his believing people in a way that is almost too much to take in. Only as we see the life of the church in the wider context of the purpose of God in redemption and as the instrument of redemption to a dying world, can we begin to appreciate why it is so important to relate within the church in a God-glorifying manner. This provides the polestar which will keep all other reflections on the unity and fellowship of the church on track.

Chapter Two

Christ's Reconciling Work
The Foundation

Architects are one thing, builders another. For a plan to move from drawing-board to concrete reality there needs to be someone willing and able to carry it out in all its detail and with all its requirements. Architects need builders and builders need architects. That is not to say that one is more important than the other, but rather that they need each other, and for the work to be accomplished there needs to be effective co-operation between them.

This brings us back into the realm of the Godhead in terms both of God's nature and the inner workings of the Trinity. Whereas it would be true to say that any Person of the Godhead – Father, Son or Holy Spirit – possesses the inherent ability to plan, execute and apply any given purpose (on account of being fully God), the very fact that God exists as Trinity means that is not the way he works. We see this fact at work in the Trinitarian involvement of God in creation. We see it supremely in the involvement of the entire Godhead in redemption.

It is no over-simplification to say that what the Father plans, the Son accomplishes and what the Son accomplishes the Spirit applies. We see this in Genesis at creation as we are immediately confronted by the eternal God (Gen. 1:1), then see his hovering Spirit – poised to enact what he decrees – (Gen. 1:2) and then hear his eternal Word (Gen. 1:3ff.). As we have said already, these facts, which are not immediately clear at the beginning of God's revelation, are explained specifically in terms of the different roles of Father, Son and Holy Spirit in creation with the progress of revelation. It is a reflection of the mystery of this Supreme Being and how he functions.

This mystery is seen even more wonderfully and with even greater significance in the workings of salvation. Going back to Ephesians for a moment, Paul has opened this great treatise with a breath-taking statement about the dimensions of salvation. (The fact that the wording of the opening statement in the original Greek runs into a staggering fourteen verses without a break says something about the captivating grandeur of this truth.) There we are confronted with the Father who has decreed the salvation of his people (Eph. 1:3-4), the Son who brought about their salvation through the shedding of his blood (Eph. 1:7), and the Holy Spirit through whom the finished work of Christ is brought into the personal experience of believers (Eph. 1:13-14). We are left in no doubt that God in the totality of his being is involved in the totality of his people's redemption. That fact must inevitably bear upon our conscious appreciation of what salvation is and how we are to see it worked out in the life and experience of the church as the people of God.

In this chapter we will spend time considering the unique and vital contribution of the Son to the work of redemption and the reunion of a divided race. As the church is seen metaphorically as a building, then Jesus is nothing less than the corner-stone of the foundation of that building, without whom it simply could not stand (Eph. 2:19-22).

Who Needs Foundations?

I never quite appreciated the importance of foundations until the small congregation I was pastoring in a church-plant erected a new building in which to meet. The smallness of our numbers meant inevitable limitations on financial resources, so we decided that to keep costs to a minimum we would do much of the physical work ourselves. (We had an unusually high proportion of skilled labour in the fellowship which made that possible.) Everyone joined in the work – minister included, despite his total lack of either skill or understanding of construction work! After having dug the trenches for the foundations and laid the concrete, I remember the evening when we were ready to start with the footings for the foundations proper. In my ignorance I expected it to be simply a matter of carrying blocks down to the bricklayers working in the trenches and before we knew it, the foundations would be in place! Not so! We seemed to spend hours taking measurements and getting levels and by the end of the evening there could hardly have been more than a couple of dozen blocks in place at the four corners of the building. My frustration was but an expression of my ignorance as the more experienced members of the work-force explained to me that unless the foundations were exactly right, the entire building would be off-skew and its stability would be in question. Foundations are important!

The same principle could not be more pertinent when it comes to the church as the spiritual edifice of the people of God. It too needs a solid foundation on which to rest, one which will give it true stability for time and eternity. It is precisely at this point that many churches have come adrift and ultimately floundered.

The foundations upon which many churches have been built have all too often been of human construction and lack the strength and durability required. In the case of many congregations and denominations their foundation has been 'our distinctives'. Undue importance has been attached to details of belief and practice which give them their particular identity. Thus the understanding of a sacrament, convictions about the style and content of worship, or subscription to a particular creed or confession have often been *the* defining elements of church life.

Variations of that kind of approach to church life can be found in the weight given to events in church history, or to the formulations of canon law. The weakness of such foundations for church life are not hard to spot. Churches which are locked into their history can easily get caught in a time warp and lose their present vitality and effectiveness, not just for a new generation of believers, but also for a fallen world which does not stand still. Likewise, churches which rely too heavily upon carefully worded statements of ecclesiastical law can soon find themselves being suffocated by a bureaucracy which is alien to a body which lives and breathes by the Spirit of God. There is a subjective element in all these 'distinctives' which makes them unreliable in themselves as foundations on which the church can be built.

At the other end of the spectrum of dangerous foundations (but which is equally subjective in its nature) is the present emphasis on experience as the defining mark of the church. The great difficulty here, of course, is that what one defines as authentic experience will be the opposite for another. The range of worship-styles which can be found within a single theologically orthodox denomination is testimony to that. To try to build stable church life and fellowship upon subjective experience is about as safe as building on quicksand!

In light of this, the significance of foundations for the unity of the church becomes clear. To attempt to build a church – either in its local expression, or collectively – on inadequate foundations is to guarantee fragmentation and mitigate against reunion. Neither baptism, psalms, history nor experience are capable of providing a foundation for the church. If the spiritual building of the people of God is to withstand the ravages of time in a hostile world, then it must rest on something which is truly secure. That can be found only in Jesus Christ and what he has done.

Objective Historical Reality

If the basis for church life and fellowship is not to be found in the realm of subjective experience, where, then, are we to find an objective reality which actually does provide cohesion and stability for the people of God? The answer must lie in something that Jesus did in his work of redemption.

It is to that great, objective, historical reality that Paul takes his readers as he speaks with confidence about the future fellowship of the church in Ephesus. The seemingly insurmountable barrier which towered between the two sections of the spiritual community – those of Jewish extraction and those from a Gentile background – was not as insurmountable as it appeared. The reason being quite simply that it had been destroyed (Eph. 2:14)! Paul's argument is that when Jesus died something happened which had a direct bearing on the experience of a divided group of people living in a different culture at a different time. They had the wherewithal to deal with their situation on the basis of what Jesus had accomplished through his death on the cross.

This explains why Paul places unique emphasis upon Christ as the cornerstone of his church. When he speaks about the foundation of this spiritual building – laid once and for all – he defines it not just in terms of 'the apostles and prophets', but the apostles and prophets locked in place by 'Christ Jesus ... the corner stone' (Eph. 2:20).

Several things are worth noting in that statement. One relates to the identity of the apostles and prophets in question and the way in which they constitute a foundation. Some have supposed, on the basis of a cursory glance at the text, that this must refer to the apostles and prophets as representing New and Old Testaments. This has an obvious appeal in that the Scriptures of the Old and New Testaments do indeed provide an objective, external basis for the existence and life of the church. But is that what Paul is saying here? Probably not. We arrive at this conclusion in part because of the word order used – why cite the New before the Old? – but more so because of the way these titles are used elsewhere in the context. The fact that Paul goes on to speak about the apostles and prophets as the Spirit's instruments of revelation 'now', making known the mystery of Christ which was 'not made known' to other generations (Eph. 3:5), clearly indicates that he has New Testament and not Old Testament prophets in mind. Paul is referring to these two offices, specific to the New Testament age, to point out that it was theirs uniquely to proclaim and explain Christ and his work as the promised Saviour of God's people: the foundation upon whom the church is built.

This is further anchored by the fact that they are set as foundation in relation to 'Christ Jesus as corner stone'. The presence of not a few false prophets and spurious apostles in New Testament times meant that the credentials of those who were genuine were in need of verification. The authenticity of a prophet or an apostle was to be found ultimately in their relation to Jesus. A true apostle was required to have been an eye-witness of the resurrected Jesus (Acts 1:22), a true prophet would of necessity confess Jesus as Lord (1 Cor. 12:3). Together they would bear witness to the uniqueness of Jesus and his work and the centrality of his death in the life of the church.

All this takes us back to one of the defining moments in the life and ministry of Jesus himself: the moment he was confessed as the Christ by Simon Peter at Caesarea Philippi (Matt. 16:16). In response to Peter's confession Jesus makes a crucial statement about the church: 'You are Peter, and upon this rock I will build My church; and the gates of Hades shall not overpower it' (Matt. 16:18).

Jesus is speaking about the way in which the church will be built and the foundation upon which it must ultimately rest, if it is not going to be overpowered by the forces of evil. Precisely what Jesus meant by this statement, however, has been one of the great enigmas with which the church has struggled throughout its history. Some have identified Peter as 'the rock' (not least on the basis of the play on words between Peter's name and the word for 'stone') and derived a doctrine of papacy. The stability of the church is to be found in an unbroken and mystical apostolic succession which can be traced back to Peter as the original vicar of Christ. Others (in part through reactionary theology) have identified 'the rock' as not Peter the man, but the confession he made. The foundation upon which Jesus will build his church has nothing to do with the fisherman from Galilee, but everything to do with his public confession of Jesus as the Christ of God.

It is hard not to think that both interpretations are wrong. Indeed, if we go back to Paul's comments to the Ephesians, we can see how he himself is drawing on what Christ said at Caesarea Philippi that day. When he speaks about the foundation upon which the church is built, he speaks about people: apostles and prophets. But he also speaks of the One whom they confess and proclaim: Christ Jesus the Lord. Most significantly, he speaks of Christ as the *crucified* Lord, as we have already seen. Surely that ties in with the fact that immediately after Jesus is acknowledged to be the Christ by Peter, he goes on to speak about the necessity of his sufferings (Matt. 16:21) – a fact to which Peter took great exception, which led to the sharpest rebuke he was ever to receive. Jesus was at pains to demonstrate that his entire mission hinged upon his suffering and with that the destiny of his church.

Tying these two threads together, then, we see how Paul is literally taking the church back to its roots: the foundation upon which it is built. He is urging the divided parties in Ephesus to look beyond that which separates them to that which unites them, and to recognize that what happened in history must have a dramatic impact upon them in their present experience in their life together.

Those who are responsible for leading the church are faced with the never-ending task of arbitration between various factions within and among congregations. The temptation is to dwell upon immediate issues, but the ultimate focus must always be the true foundation upon which we rest: the finished work of Christ upon the cross. There and there alone was true reconciliation secured and from there exclusively can true reconciliation be derived.

The Dimensions of Reconciliation

As we look more closely at the way Paul unpacks this amazing event, we begin to appreciate precisely what happened and how it relates to the situation in Ephesus. The event upon which Paul is focusing our thoughts is clearly the death of Jesus upon the cross. He is addressing the Gentile believers in the church in Ephesus and explaining to them how they, who were once alienated from God and his promises, have now been brought near. The key is, they 'have been brought near by the blood of Christ' (Eph. 2:13). Their entitlement to a place in God's covenant community rests exclusively upon the death of Christ. This in turn affects how they relate to others in the same community.

The critical axis in this complex of relationships is on the vertical plane. At one time these Gentiles were doubly alienated from God: primarily on account of their fallen nature, but ceremonially because they were outside the visible community of God's ancient people, the Jews. They had 'no hope' and were 'without God in the world' (Eph. 2:12). But Jesus had dealt with that alienation in both respects through his death on Calvary. He, through his blood, had brought these believing Gentiles near to God – he personally made peace on their behalf with God (Eph. 2:13-14). As the veil in the temple was supernaturally torn in two (Mark 15:38), the way into the immediate presence of God was symbolically thrown open for all.

The twist in the tail of what Paul is saying here is that

although he seems to be directly addressing those of Gentile extraction, he is actually speaking to the converted Jews at the same time. As they listen in to his comments with undoubted smug satisfaction at the distance there was between the Gentiles and God, it must have come as no small shock to their system to hear that God's way of bringing Jews near to him was no different from his way of bringing in the Gentiles! It is the same Jesus who brings Jews into peace with God (Eph. 2:14) and the same Jesus who reconciles the Gentile to God as well (Eph. 2:16).

The basis of salvation is the same for both. As they stood on level ground before God in their need, so they stand on level ground before him in their salvation. Only Christ through his death could meet the needs of both.

Having shown how God restored the vertical axis of their fallen state through the death of Christ, Paul goes on to see how that affects their relationships on the horizontal axis. In particular, how they now relate to those against whom they had a sinful prejudice prior to their conversion. That too falls under the transforming shadow of the crucified Saviour. His death meant the death of the enmity that once existed between these two groups themselves and between both groups and God (Eph. 2:16).

That was true at a ceremonial level (Eph. 2:15) in the sense that Old Testament Jewish ceremonial law did indeed exclude Gentiles from the privileges of outward communion with God through the temple ordinances – there was an actual wall in the temple precincts confining non-Jews to the court of the Gentiles and excluding them from the place of intimate fellowship with God. The death of Jesus brought an end to those ceremonial requirements of the Old Covenant system. That barrier was removed.

But even deeper still, Jesus dealt with that sinful animosity that not only set man against God, but man against man as well. His death was nothing less than God's instrument for producing a new humanity in which people are drawn from all sides of a fragmented race and are made fellow-citizens and fellow-members in God's household of faith (Eph. 2:19).

The beauty of what Paul is doing here lies in the fact that he not only shows how reconciliation was secured through the death of Christ, but also how it is applied and worked out in practice. In the same way as reconciliation to God is experienced through looking in faith to the cross (the place where the reconciling transaction happened), so reconciliation between men is effected by looking to that same cross (where the same transaction had a bearing upon such relationships). Thus, as Paul was urging both Jew and Gentile in Ephesus to look beyond what made them different to the Christ who made them one, so in every generation of the church and in every manifestation of division, true reconciliation comes only through focus on Christ. This is true both forensically in terms of where we stand in relation to each other, but also in terms of how we feel and function.

The Dynamics of Reconciliation
The death of Christ meant far more than simply a new standing for sinners before God: it secured a new relationship. Thus, as the death of Jesus is remembered sacramentally in the life of the church, it is in an act of communion. In a tangible way which involves all five senses we see again how communion with God was restored through the sacrifice of his Son. Indeed, for many

believers, some of the sweetest moments of spiritual experience have been found in that act around the Lord's table. It is a graphic illustration of the way in which the forensic and the experimental aspects of the work of Christ belong together for those who love him. It is in precisely the same location and the same event that this truth touches upon the relationships between his children as well.

The men of the Westminster Assembly captured it quite exquisitely in their wording of the Confession's chapter, 'on the Communion of Saints':[5]

> All saints that are united to Jesus Christ their head by his Spirit, and by faith, have fellowship with him in his graces, sufferings, death, resurrection, and glory. And being united to one another in love, they have communion in each other's gifts and graces.

In other words, union and communion with Christ means union and communion with his people. The vertical and horizontal planes of Christian fellowship are inseparable.

The practical impact of this doctrine upon fellowship within churches and fellowship between churches ought to be enormous. Where there is a recognition of true kinship in Christ, it will of necessity lead to genuine efforts to cultivate the bond of fellowship that has been established. Where other barriers have existed on account of our fallenness, we will apply ourselves, in Christ and by his Spirit, to removing them. The lingering effects of sin and the sheer strength of so many of the obstacles will mean that the task will never be easy, but the obligation we have to each other, in Christ and for his sake, brings it into sharp focus.

So, whether it be the need to bridge the divide between racially distinct church groupings, or congregations with a socially disparate make-up, or even situations where inadequate understanding of Scripture has blurred theology in general; where there is unmistakable recognition of Christ as Saviour and Lord, there is relationship and there is responsibility. Likewise, where there have been wounds from the divisions of the past, in Christ we have the obligation to acknowledge past sin and failure – not just to God, but to each other – in order that guilt might be removed, wounds healed and reconciliation achieved.

A sad indictment upon those who have been theologically strong in the history of the church is that they have not always been as pastorally concerned as they ought. Rather than adopt the posture of Priscilla and Aquila, showing an erring brother 'the way of God more accurately' (Acts 18:26), they have opted instead for a spiritual version of apartheid. Only when we appreciate the price paid for the bonds of fellowship to be established between God and his people and among his people themselves can we truly grasp why, as Paul says, no effort must be spared, no stone left unturned in the preservation of the unity of the Spirit established in the bond of peace (Eph. 4:3).

Chapter Three

The Spirit's Unifying Power
The Wherewithal to Build

It must surely be both one of the greatest ironies as well as one of the greatest tragedies of the twentieth century that the doctrine of the Holy Spirit has become one of the greatest causes of division within the church. The third Person of the Godhead, who is identified so directly with the unity of God's people (Eph. 4:3), has become the pretext for disunity on an enormous scale throughout the world. The sheer incongruity of that fact in itself ought to be enough to send us all back to the Scriptures to explore again what they say about the Spirit's role in establishing the unity of the church. To develop the imagery of the spiritual building site: it is God the Holy Spirit who gives us the wherewithal to construct this spiritual edifice of the household of faith.

Once again it is striking that it is in the epistle to the Ephesians that Paul taps into the rich vein of theological truth which undergirds the fellowship of the saints. There he demonstrates the unique contribution made by God's Spirit in this critical aspect of Christian living. He demonstrates in a most persuasive and challenging way how the Spirit of God becomes the empowering presence of God in the corporate as well as the individual life of his people. He actually enables them to overcome the sinful instincts with which they are born and the sinful patterns of behaviour to which they are constantly exposed in this fallen world.

The importance of this for the Ephesian church is clear. The people in those congregations were struggling with a deep-rooted problem. Humanly speaking they were faced with an impossible task in trying to resolve it. So, to be told that there was divine provision for this particular need must have come as a tremendous comfort and encouragement to them all – on both sides of the ecclesiastical divide which had emerged.

That same truth provides hope and encouragement for believers in all ages, facing all kinds of disunity. We have not been left orphan-like to cope with deep-seated and painful problems like these with mere human wisdom and resources. God in his love and grace has equipped the saints with all they need, not just to face such difficulties, but to overcome them in a way which makes a dramatic statement to the world about the reality of his salvation.

If we turn to the passage at the beginning of the fourth chapter of Ephesians which takes up the issue of the Spirit's work in establishing unity among God's people, we see that Paul works backwards from exhortation: '... walk in a manner worthy of the calling with which you have been called ...' (verse 1), to basis: 'There is one body and one Spirit ...' (verse 4). To appreciate the full force of the apostle's line of reasoning, we might do well to approach it in reverse, considering first the provision God has made through the Holy Spirit and then seeing how that allows for God to make bold and seemingly impossible demands on his people with regard to their conduct in the church and in the world.

The Spirit and the Body

The existence of the church as the body of Christ and the work of the Holy Spirit as God's agent in redemption are inseparable. The unity of God's purpose and the integral nature of each component with all the others are evident from Paul's emphasis on all that is 'one' in the outworking of God's salvation:

> There is one body and one Spirit, just as also you were called in one hope of your calling; one Lord, one faith, one baptism, one God and Father of all who is over all and through all and in all (Eph. 4:4-6).

The very tone of that statement says something about its magnitude. It is a regal comment about God, his purpose and his people. It straddles his saving purpose between the Testaments. The people of God in the days before Christ were saved in a way that was no different from those saved since his coming. There are not two bodies or two peoples with two distinct destinies; they are one people who share the prospect of the same glory to come through the same Messiah: Jesus Christ.

The statement in Ephesians 4 has something rather poignant to say to the believers in Ephesus. Their behaviour towards each other was such that it gave the impression at least that there were really two churches, or at best one church with first and second class citizens within it. This, then, was a direct challenge to their mindset and their conduct – it was quite simply inconsistent with all that God had done among them (and his people everywhere) by his Son and through his Spirit.

The role of the Spirit in the establishment of the church went far deeper than many of these people had imagined.

He was present and active at every point, both in bringing them into the family of God and in building them up in their faith and fellowship. Quite simply, they could not account for their existence as a church, or understand what that entailed without reference to the Spirit.

It is the Spirit who works in the heart of a sinner prior to conversion. Paul has already alluded to this in the second chapter when he spoke of the Ephesians being 'dead' in 'trespasses and sins' (Eph. 2:1), needing ultimately to be 'made ... alive together with Christ' (Eph. 2:5). Even though there is no specific reference to the Holy Spirit in those statements, there is no question but that it is the Spirit Paul has in mind. It calls to mind the detailed instruction Jesus gave and John recorded in his gospel concerning the Spirit's work in regeneration, conversion and sanctification.

The stark nature of the plight of our human condition was set bluntly before Nicodemus the Pharisee in his memorable encounter with Jesus. His fundamental problem was his need of life! Jesus told this man in no uncertain terms, 'unless one is born again, he cannot see the kingdom of God' (John 3:3). Until such times as this religious man received life which was 'from above' (the word translated 'again' carries the overtones of 'from above') he was incapable of 'seeing', that is, actually experiencing what it was like to be part of God's kingdom. On one hand such news must have been quite devastating for a man who had applied himself devoutly to religious exercises for his hope of salvation, but on the other hand it must have come as a great relief. For the first time he was hearing something which explained the hollowness of his religious experience. He was learning the truth that his need went far beyond his capabilities as a fallen human being.

The beauty of what Jesus had to say to this man was that he did not merely diagnose his problem, he pointed to the provision God had made in his more than adequate salvation. He goes on to explain precisely how this life 'from above' is received and experienced by those who are still below. It is only those who are born 'of water and of the Spirit' (John 3:5) who will enter the kingdom.

The moment, then, at which a person passes from spiritual death to spiritual life is a moment which is under the Holy Spirit's sovereign control. The dead cannot raise themselves. Those who have no life by nature are incapable of receiving it by themselves. But at that crucial point of need God's Holy Spirit is at work. Thus, when he performs his work of convicting of sin, righteousness and judgement (John 16:8-11) in the lives of such people, it will manifest itself ultimately in faith and repentance. Having been brought to an end of themselves, they are brought by the Spirit to Jesus and to the full salvation he alone provides.

Those who are truly God's people have experienced the same workings of God's Spirit in their lives in conversion. There is no room for pride or discrimination in terms of how a person enters that new relationship with God through Jesus Christ. It is the same Spirit who works in all. Thus where there is evidence of new birth shown in a Spirit-renewed life, there is an obligation to acknowledge what God has done and strive to pursue what God desires in the corporate life of his family.

It should not surprise us that the Spirit who incorporates us into the body of Christ also sustains us in that body and continues the work begun in regeneration and conversion until it is carried through to completion in glorification. The Spirit who brings people to faith in Christ is the same

Spirit who resides in those who have faith in Christ (Rom.
8:9). He indwells them individually in such a way that their
bodies are regarded as his holy temple and thus must be
used in a manner commensurate with such an exalted
resident (1 Cor. 6:19-20). These truths cannot but have a
profound effect on the way we understand ourselves as
believers. Even though we are faced with requirements and
expectations from God concerning our conduct which to
us seem beyond the realm of what we are able to do, we
are willing to attempt and even accomplish through the
power the Spirit imparts to us. This, of course, makes
nonsense of the excuse we so often put up in the face of
God's demands upon us: 'But we cannot do it!' Although
that objection was certainly valid in our pre-conversion
days, it is no longer valid since our incorporation into
Christ. The significance of that in terms of how we relate
personally to those with whom we have differences of one
sort or another is quite devastating. Too many disputes and
differences have been left unresolved on the pretext of there
being 'nothing we can do about it'. Such excuses simply
do not hold water in the sight of God and he will hold us
accountable for our unwillingness – as opposed to inability
– to do what he expects of us.

The presence and work of the Spirit in the church has a
dimension greater than that expressed in the lives of
individual Christians. It is interesting to note that Paul has
already spoken of the 'temple of the Holy Spirit' in another
place in his letter to the Corinthians, just a little bit before
the reference we have already mentioned. Having spoken
about the church in the metaphorical language of a building
site, Paul says:

> Do you not know that you [plural] are a temple of God, and that
> the Spirit of God dwells in you? If any man destroys the temple of
> God, God will destroy him, for the temple of God is holy, and that
> is what you are (1 Cor. 3:16-17).

Such a comment was particularly pertinent to the
situation in the church at Corinth which was being torn
apart by various petty factions within the fellowship (1
Cor. 1:11-13). The temple of God in that place was indeed
being destroyed in terms of its visible unity and the
testimony which depended upon that. Thus Paul had to
remind the Christians in that community that there was a
corporate dimension to their Christian life and the work of
God's Spirit among them which could not be overlooked
or ignored. The Spirit proves his power and presence not
just in individual lives but in the collective experience of
God's children as they live together as his people.

Paul's exhortation to the church in Philippi (which also
had trouble with internal wrangling and divisions) brings
this out with some force when he says,

> So then, my beloved, just as you have always obeyed, not as in my
> presence only, but now much more in my absence, work out your
> salvation with fear and trembling; for it is God who is at work in
> you, both to will and to work for His good pleasure (Phil. 2:12-
> 13).

One of the most striking things about that well-known
comment is that it is couched in plural language. Although
it is obviously a call to grow in grace and make progress in
the faith, it is not merely aimed at individuals and private
conduct, rather it is directed towards the corporate
responsibility of the family of God. Spiritual maturity is
not truly manifest in terms of outstanding saints in the

church of Christ, but instead through corporate
congregational (and inter-congregational) life which is
measured by collective progress in the faith.

It is as that responsibility is abdicated, either by
individuals within a church, or by supercilious churches
within the wider fellowship of churches, that the testimony
of the church is so badly marred. It is sad to see situations
develop where enormous risks are taken by those who dare
to venture outside particular spiritual or theological
stockades simply to talk with those who profess to share
the same *Evangel*, but who have different emphases. Yet
if we take seriously Christ's commendation of those who
are 'peacemakers' (Matt. 5:9) – especially if they are
concerned with peace within the household of faith – then
there ought to be more who are prepared to take such risks
for the peace of God's kingdom.

The Spirit's presence, power and work in the church is
such that its unity is rightly called 'the unity *of* the Spirit'
(Eph. 4:3). It is a given. It is there by virtue of the Spirit's
being there. It is not something that can be artificially
manufactured or maintained, but, as it is dependent upon
the Spirit for its origin, so it must depend on him for its
sustenance. As such, it is something of enormous worth
and in need of being cherished and guarded by those to
whom it has been given.

Spiritual Unity Under Threat
Paul's instruction to his Ephesian hearers to invest their
best efforts in the preservation of that spiritual unity alerts
them and us to the fact that it is under threat. Although the
two factions in the situation in Ephesus were in a sense
focused on the surface issues of their respective views on

what was necessary for authentic Christian experience, there was a deeper issue at stake – the unity of the body of Christ. The damage that would be caused through impairing that precious commodity in any way would be far worse than the damage perceived to be caused by these other concerns.

The significance of this need in the corporate life of God's people is no new thing. We find it stated powerfully and eloquently in the Old Testament in the memorable words of one of the Songs of Ascents – psalms associated with the great pilgrimages of God's people to the festal gatherings in Jerusalem on the holy days throughout the year. Jerusalem itself became the symbolic focus of the people of God. Despite their diversity, coming as they did from the various tribes and the different regions of the land, they were able to express their oneness in the city of Zion, in communion with their God and Saviour. Thus there was sincerity and passion in their prayer,

> Pray for the peace of Jerusalem;
> 'May they prosper who love you.
> 'May peace be within your walls,
> And prosperity within your palaces.'
> For the sake of my brothers and my friends,
> I will now say, 'May peace be within you.'
> For the sake of the house of the LORD our God
> I will seek your good (Ps. 122:6-9).

The way in which that prayer is expressed is in itself interesting and ties in remarkably with Paul's sentiment in the Ephesian passage.

We are confronted with something of a mystery in both these passages. On the one hand we are reminded of the sovereignty of the Spirit of God in the unity of his people. As we have seen already, the unity they enjoy is not something of human origin, or which has been manufactured by men, rather it is something which has been divinely bestowed. It seems almost incongruous therefore to imagine that it could ever be threatened in any way, or that human beings could in any sense protect what comes from God.

This mystery is, of course, but another expression of the twin truths of divine sovereignty and human responsibility set before us in the Word of God. Trying to contain the relationship between the two within the confines of finite, fallen human logic is an impossible task, yet the very fact that God has chosen to reveal himself and his workings in this way impresses upon us the need to take each truth seriously in itself and be prepared to live with the tension which arises from their being placed side by side in Scripture.

The emphasis upon divine sovereignty provides the basis of confidence in it all: the security and unity of the people of God are undergirded by the unshakeable purpose of Almighty God. The stress on human responsibility calls for willing compliance on the part of his people to the revelation of his will and purpose. It has been the need to hold these two truths in balance which has so often proved difficult in the life of the church. There has been an instinctive desire to lean more to one side than to the other, but to do either is to undermine the comfort of the gospel.

This imbalance in relation to maintaining unity within the church has manifest itself either in a somewhat fatalistic approach to divisive problems which simply says, 'We must pray for revival', or else in an attempt to immerse the church in all kinds of schemes for unity. Neither fatalism, nor activism can ever bring about the effective unity of which both the psalmist and the apostle are speaking.

Instead we are being called, in the psalm, both to 'pray for' and actively and constructively 'seek' the corporate well-being of God's people; and in the epistle, both to acknowledge the unity is there by God's grace and to pursue it energetically in obedience to God's command. It is only possible to cope with that tension as we live by faith in Jesus Christ and through him begin to experience the restoration of the true humanity for which God created us; a humanity which lives in communion with the sovereign God, but functions with a will and faculties which are in voluntary submission to him.

If we translate that into the practical concerns of 'seeking the peace of Jerusalem' – the unity of the church – it must mean that we will both pray and labour to that end. We will indeed pray for revival. Unless the sovereign Lord pours out his gracious Spirit upon the lives of his own people in renewal and sanctification, and upon the world in converting power, the disintegrating effects of sin will persist and multiply. However, at the same time, we will labour for reformation within the church, a reformation which not only touches the way we confess our faith, but also the way that faith is applied in godly, corporate Christian living. The responsibility of each constitutes a major challenge in its own right.

The unity of the Spirit among the true people of God is a wonderful reality of grace, but one which can never be taken for granted. As it was in the beginning that the arch-enemy of God and of his people was bent on destroying God's good creation, so in the present that same enemy is bent on disrupting his new creation in the Lord Jesus Christ. All who are part of that new creation need to appreciate the threat he poses and guard what God has entrusted to us for his glory.

The Spirit Equips God's People for Unity

As we continue tracing Paul's reasoning back from what God has ordained in his eternal purpose, through what God has established through his Son and his Spirit, we come next to what God has provided for his people in order to work this out in practice. Hence we see that the kind of conduct which God calls for in his family is conduct characterized by the fruit of the Spirit, all of which have a bearing on relationships within the church (Eph. 4:2). The specific needs we face as we struggle with sin-damaged relationships are specifically provided for in Christ-redeemed relationships by his Spirit.

Thus where by nature we are arrogant and proud in ourselves, the Spirit grants the grace of 'humility'; where sin has created insensitive belligerence, the Spirit creates a Christ-like gentleness; where there is self-centred petulance, in salvation there comes a patience that is prepared to wait in faith on God; intolerance is exchanged for tolerance and all these graces are wrapped up in love! The totality and sufficiency of the Holy Spirit's provision are quite remarkable.

To see these particular traits applied and worked out in the lives of the believers caught up in the painful conflict in Ephesus could not have been more appropriate. The apostle refuses to ignore the problem that was tearing the very heart out of that fellowship; he addresses it head-on, but in a way that demonstrates God's perfect provision for all the factors which were making the issue into the problem that it was among them.

The very essence of the antagonism felt by the Jewish converts in Ephesus towards their non-Jewish brothers and sisters was expressed in the kind of sinful attitudes met by the Spirit's antidote. There was a nationalistic pride which revelled in their ethnic identity and looked down upon others who did not share it. There was a violent and intrusive spirit that was prepared to foist the cultural requirements of their Jewish-ness upon those who were non-Jews. Far from being characterized by patience and tolerance, their relationship with these Gentile converts with whom they shared the church was quite the opposite, hence the crisis-point they were reaching and the firm apostolic rebuke it was receiving. The very trait which was uniquely intended to distinguish these people as followers of Christ – their love for one another (John 13:35) – was strikingly absent.

There is, without question, no worse form of fuel to pour on the fires of disagreement within the church and between churches than that of arrogance, aggression, impatience and intolerance. No matter how strong our convictions may be, nor how strong our feelings in particular areas, there must be a Christ-like spirit which enables us to conduct our disputes in a manner which does not dishonour the name of our Saviour. Such grace can only be ours through the Spirit of Christ who dwells in his people and who can produce such fruit in their lives and in their fellowship.

The Spirit's Calling for the Church

Speaking to the Christians in Galatia (who happened to be facing a similar problem to that encountered in Ephesus), Paul says, 'Walk by the Spirit' (Gal. 5:25), or, as it can also be translated, 'Keep in step with the Spirit'. What he means is that the Holy Spirit provides the pattern and sets the pace for God's people, and their duty before God is quite simply to follow him. The exhortation Paul gives to their Ephesian counterparts is really no different, 'Walk in a manner worthy of the calling with which you have been called' (Eph. 4:1). The bottom line of this redemptive equation is a conscious response from those who have truly been redeemed. It is not enough to theorize and theologize about the provision God has made in the gospel, it must translate into practice through transformed lives and transformed relationships.

The breath-taking truths about God and his plan, Christ and his sacrifice and the Holy Spirit and his power are earthed by the apostle in the day-to-day reality of his people and their conduct. If salvation has been genuinely experienced, it must be seen in new God-centred obedience in place of the old God-denying rebellion.

God pursues his transforming purpose in the lives of his people by engaging them and seeking a conscious response from them. The outworking of their salvation is not something in which they are passive, but rather vibrantly active. Their ability to respond to God's overtures, as we have seen, derives directly from the presence and work of his Spirit within them, but that does not minimize the fact that they themselves are responding to God in real obedience. God allows them to experience the inner struggle of wrestling with the temptations of an old way of life consistent with their old nature, but he does so in order to prove the reality of the new nature they possess in Christ by being able to behave in an altogether different way.

As that same challenging exhortation is set before the church of every generation, we are reminded of the high calling we have in the family of God. A calling which summons us to rise above the old divided order of a fallen divided world. Yet so often it is precisely at that point that we can become deaf to God's command. We do not allow his calling to interfere with our own particular stance.

Although it is right and necessary for us as Christians and as churches to hold clear and firm convictions, we must hold them in such a way as to distinguish between convictions over truths which are non-negotiable and convictions over truths which are. Paul himself indicates a distinction to be made between doctrines which are 'of first importance' (1 Cor. 15:3) and those which by definition are to be regarded as secondary. When we try to elevate subordinate truth to the level of cardinal truth, we not only damage the church, we damage the gospel. But as well as that, we need to hold our convictions in a way that constantly allows them and us to be interrogated by the Word of God itself and kept in line with God's supreme rule for faith and life.

The frightening ease with which even the best of churches can be blown off course in this area is seen in the slide of many evangelical churches into Protestant scholasticism in the nineteenth century. It is almost unbelievable to see the shift which took place in the English-speaking world from the theological precision, evangelical warmth and missionary zeal that characterized the seventeenth and eighteenth centuries to the arid and moribund scholastic religion of the nineteenth century. The point at which the imbalance came in has been well expressed in the dictum, 'In the seventeenth century the church confessed her beliefs, in the eighteenth, she believed her confessions.'

What happened on a large scale in the evangelical world in that era has been the perennial threat to evangelical churches of every era. They can easily end up with a system-faith which is cut adrift from the living Word of God that shapes both doctrine itself and the way in which doctrines are held, and also cut adrift from the Spirit of God who alone provides the wherewithal to construct a truly united fellowship among the saints.

Summary
True and meaningful unity must of necessity begin with God and not with men – even those who are redeemed. So much fragmentation has been caused and so many attempts at reunion have foundered because that order has been reversed. The unity of the church, as much as any other aspect of its life, comes under the sovereign lordship of the Triune God.

The ultimate purpose of God the Father, the ultimate achievement of God the Son and the end-point of God the Holy Spirit's sanctifying work is that in the corporate life of God's people they shall be perfectly one.

Despite all the failures, frustrations and disappointments we experience in this world and in this present age, the future oneness of the church is guaranteed by divine decree and accomplishment. But insofar as the church is comprised of those who 'have tasted ... the powers of the age to come'

(Heb. 6:4-5), that future certainty only becomes present possibility and reality the more we look to God.

By making God, as opposed to unity, our focus, we are not only encouraged in the face of what appears to be the impossible, we are also impelled, in dependence upon Christ and his Spirit and obedience to God and his command, to pursue this enriching fellowship of the saints which is bound up with the very essence of salvation. The God to whom we look and upon whom we depend will then lead us by the means he has provided to make that union and communion an experimental reality in the life of the church.

Chapter Four

Biblical Constraint
The Defining and Controlling Influence of Scripture

The painful paradox of evangelical unity is that its very aspiration to be evangelical is simultaneously its greatest help and its greatest hindrance. It is obviously the former (as we have hinted already) because the only way to guarantee a unity which is authentic and which truly pleases God is to allow it to be shaped by his Word. But then it can become the latter when we get down to the nitty-gritty of defining the precise biblical character of what it means to be evangelical. That need for definition suffers at both ends of the spectrum. At one end it is increasingly apparent that what it means to be an evangelical is so loosely linked with Scripture that an adjective which involves a reference to the *Evangel* becomes a nonsense. At the other end of the spectrum damage is done by those who are over-fastidious in their desire to be faithful to the Bible. They engage in a modern equivalent of the pharisaical practice of 'fencing the Law'. That is, in a zealous desire to ensure that obedience to God's law is faithful, they construct a 'fence' out of their own laws and traditions which are beyond the scope of Scripture to be doubly sure that the limits set by the Bible are not infringed. Although the fervour for faithfulness in such zeal is in one sense laudable, the fact that Christ himself castigates such people as setting aside the commandment of God in order to keep their own tradition (Mark 7:9) casts it in a different light. The seriousness of that rebuke from our Lord ought not to be minimized, not least because it is directed against the kind of people who least expect to hear it. Somehow it is perceived that being over-zealous could not be a sin, while its opposite so manifestly is. Perhaps surprisingly we find Jesus being much more patient with those who fall into the latter category rather than the former.

Either way, it is clear that Scripture has a vital role to play in shaping and achieving a meaningful unity among believers and we can never afford to neglect the need to approach it in a way that will lead to a faithful understanding of what it says.

The Role of Interpretation

Straightaway this need brings us into what has been the focus and battleground of recent evangelical history. Hermeneutics – the technical term for the principles of interpretation – have become 'the epicentre of current theological conflict'. In part this reflects the sea-change, or paradigm-shift, that has overtaken modern western thinking in general. The whole concept of words and meaning has undergone radical revision so that it has become increasingly difficult to define and control how people think. The very notions of absolutes and authority have been all but abandoned and the forces of relativism and pluralism have taken their place. One graduate of Harvard University is reputed to have said on the day of his graduation, 'In this institution you are free to believe whatever you want, so long as it is not true!' It is not politically correct to believe anything which pretends to be the norm for more than just the individual. The consequences of this mindset, in terms of the fluidity and fragmentation in the secular world, are frightening to observe, but the rot of that destructive outlook on life is not confined to what is secular.

The nerve-centre of evangelical Christianity is the way it views and understands the Bible. Its fundamental tenet, the presupposition upon which it rests, must be the assertion, 'The Bible is the Word of God'. That alone safeguards the objectivity of the foundation of faith and preserves it from the subjectivism which is inevitably contaminated by the fallenness of the world in which we live. So vital is this assertion that we are not surprised to find that it has come under relentless attack throughout the ages and especially in recent centuries since the Enlightenment. From the blatant denials by Liberal scepticism that the Bible is the Word of God, to the more subtle approach found in Neo-orthodoxy of the Bible simply *containing* the Word of God, right down to the contemporary onslaught on what is meant by the concept 'Word of God' in itself, the foundation of the Faith has been under persistent attack.

As soon as our understanding of the nature of Scripture is damaged – by whatever means – then there is an inevitable string of casualties which will fall in its wake. If we move away from viewing it ultimately as God's Word (without in any sense taking away from its real human characteristics), or if we try to redefine what that means, then the next step is to question its authority, reliability and sufficiency in what it says about faith and life. Yet this is precisely where so many who still want to operate under an evangelical banner find themselves. They want to claim the credentials of the *Evangel* without being bound by its inherent requirements. That has had (and continues to have) inevitable bitter consequences for fellowship within the evangelical community.

Our view of the nature of Scripture has a bearing upon the related task of interpretation. What principles need to be applied in order to bridge the cultural, geographical and historical gulf that exists between the world of the Bible and the world of its readers? Throughout the history of the church a variety of principles has been invoked for this task and a significant measure of evolution is evident as the strengths and weaknesses of different approaches have been worked through. The controlling principle of interpretation which came to the fore at the time of the Reformation and which has exercised the greatest influence in mainstream evangelicalism was what has come to be known as the grammatico-historical method. This is simply an approach which seeks to establish the plain meaning of the text in the light of its grammar and historical setting. Such a view of the method of interpretation produced considerable agreement between Christians over the central message of the Bible.

It was only as changes in the theory of words and their meaning in the secular world began to encroach significantly upon evangelical scholarship in the middle part of the twentieth century that the evangelical consensus on the central meaning of Scripture began to change.

It is hardly surprising that the emergence of what became known as 'the New Hermeneutic' in evangelical circles began to put strain on fellowship within those circles. Basic agreement on the nature of the foundation of that fellowship (which allowed for considerable diversity in the detail of belief and practice) was lost and the fellowship itself began to suffer within the evangelical family on both sides of the Atlantic. The way we view Scripture and how we interpret Scripture will of necessity affect the way we are able to unite around Scripture.

Holding Hands in the Dark

Some years ago the whole thrust of the ecumenical movement in Britain took a new turn. Having followed for years the pattern set by the *World Council of Churches* of trying to establish unity by means of committees and bureaucracy – unity from the top down – it turned its attention to the grass-roots of churches themselves. What emerged was a movement under the title of *Churches Together* which simply sought to encourage local churches to meet together and co-operate in different ventures regardless of their denominational or credal distinctives. This new departure in ecumenism was remarkably successful, coming at a time when many were losing heart with the bureaucratic approach of professional ecumenists and when the accelerating decline in church attendance made many churches aware of their need for wider local contact purely for their survival. However, its apparent strength and reason for its success was (and continues to be) its actual weakness. That is, its view of truth.

The most vocal and constructive criticism of this venture came from evangelicals involved with the *British Evangelical Council* – an inter-church group representing some 1,200 conservative evangelical congregations. The title they gave to their most effective and popular pamphlet responding to this new move was *Holding Hands in the Dark*. It pointed out that apparent unity was being achieved at the expense of significant sacrifice. Those who were involving themselves in this co-operation were prepared to set aside much of what they believed in order to relate to others in something that was only very loosely Christian.

Sadly, that route to unity which was seized by many non-evangelicals in Britain in the 1980s has become the preferred route for their evangelical counterparts since then. A minimalist approach to defining what a church believes, moving away from historic creeds and confessions towards more concise and fluid statements of faith, has left many in the evangelical world 'holding hands in the dark' as well.

For unity to have meaning and substance it must be 'in the truth'. There is a desperate need to recover on the one hand, a high view of what the Bible is, and on the other hand, a sane and reasonable approach to establishing what it says and means. The fact that the former is under subtle attack from within the professing evangelical community is evident from pressure to put other forms of revelation alongside Scripture. Regardless of how one tries to define and qualify these other forms of divine, direct communication, they have the sole effect of displacing the Bible from its central place in the life of the church. The influence of Pentecostal and Charismatic theology at this point has been significant and the issues that it has raised cannot be ducked in the quest for real and meaningful unity among God's people. Whereas it is undoubtedly the case that there can be and indeed is genuine fellowship between those who believe in continuing forms of revelation and those who do not, there is a world of a difference in theological terms between fostering that fellowship informally and institutionalizing it in some form of defined fellowship. It does not require a prophetic gift to say that for present-day evangelicals this is the most important issue that needs to be addressed as it is bound to have a profound impact upon the shape of evangelicalism for the foreseeable future.

The need to recover a sane approach to hermeneutics is no less important. Every principle of interpretation that we apply to God's Word must be designed to let Scripture speak plainly for itself rather than to try to squeeze it into a form with which its readers feel more comfortable. Too many hermeneutical tools in today's evangelical world have the effect of gagging the Bible rather than allowing it to speak. Hence the terrifying moral and spiritual confusion which has invaded numerous churches.

Finding the Balance

How can we recover some degree of sanity in our approach to Scripture as the basis of our fellowship in Christ? The answer is surely to be found from within Scripture itself. As we look at the obvious diversity that existed among God's people, especially in the New Testament, we need to ask what it was that prevented diversity from being turned into division.

The answer in part must lie in the ability of New Testament believers to distinguish between primary and secondary doctrine. The apostle Paul alludes to that distinction as he addresses Christians in a church setting which was wracked by factions and division in Corinth. As he approaches the theological heart of his epistle, drawing his readers' attention to truths which were non-negotiable, he says:

> For I delivered to you as of first importance what I also received,
> that Christ died for our sins according to the Scriptures, and that
> He was buried and that He was raised on the third day according to
> the Scriptures and that He appeared to Cephas, then to the twelve
> (1 Cor. 15:3-5).

Here were cardinal truths: doctrines on which the Christian
faith would either stand or fall. As the Corinthian church
struggled with internal pressures and tensions which
threatened to explode its fellowship, Paul seeks to anchor
it in those truths which underpin its very existence. His
approach is a vital antidote to the reckless spirit which was
taking over and which had shifted the focus of that
congregation to non-essentials. Churches today, in this age
of fragmentation, have an even greater need to restore a
biblically balanced focus on what it is that makes us
Christians.

The obvious reason for so many of the divisions within
the church over the centuries is the fact that issues which
are secondary in Scripture have been elevated to the level
of primary importance. Thus, as has been indicated already,
differing views on baptism or forms of worship have
become pretexts for exclusion from fellowship. In light of
what Paul says, it is clear that since salvation cannot rest
on either of those issues (or others which fall into similar
categories), God's people should not allow them to impede
meaningful fellowship between them.

The practical implications of this are enormous. At the
most basic level we are forced to re-examine the ultimate
foundation for faith and practice within the church. While
most professing evangelicals would readily affirm that the
Word of God, which is comprised of the Scriptures of the
Old and New Testaments, is the only infallible rule for

faith and life, what they mean by that is not always clear in practice.

Some churches, which place a strong emphasis on creeds and confessions as the summary of what they believe, have allowed them in effect to displace the Bible from its unique place in the life of the church. Even though they make a distinction between the Word of God as the supreme standard for faith and life and their statements of faith as subordinate standards, all too often that which is meant to have a secondary role is in reality allowed to become primary. No matter how clear and accurate catechisms, creeds and confessions may be, they are only human documents and they do not possess the authority, sufficiency and reliability which is exclusive to Scripture. The watershed that marked the decline of churches into Protestant scholasticism, referred to above,[6] has been repeated on a smaller scale with alarming frequency in the history of conservative evangelical churches. To allow that to happen in any generation is to sound the death-knell, not just for the life of a particular church, but for the wider fellowship it might enjoy with other churches. The very documents which ought to be an expression of biblical truth and an aid to genuine fellowship can become an impossible handicap. The line which marks off such confessional statements from disturbing the sufficiency of Scripture is a fine one.

The sufficiency of Scripture can also be undermined from another quarter within the evangelical community, a sector to which we have alluded already and which has arguably become the dominant grouping within evangelicalism. We are talking here, of course, of that sector which holds to some form of continuing prophecy within the church. Strenuous efforts have been made by scholars such as Wayne Grudem to posit a view of continuing prophecy which should not be regarded as special revelation and is therefore non-canonical.[7] The danger of such a view of prophecy lies not only in the weakness of the exegetical base on which it rests, but in the weakness of the human psychology of those to whom it is delivered. The practice of conservative churches which espouse some form of this understanding of prophecy is often to provide some point in public worship during which 'prophecies' can be delivered. Even though such times may well not displace the sermon either in terms of time allocation, or even their place in the order of service, the psychological effect is invariably the same. The congregation is on the edge of its seat wondering, 'What is God going to say to us *today*?' Human hunger for the immediate, the very concept of some form of 'hot-line to heaven', leaves even the best attempts to expound Scripture looking dull by comparison to what 'the prophet' will say for the week. The overall impact is to leave God's people with the sense that the Bible is not enough.

Where the centrality and sufficiency of Scripture is undermined from either quarter, the foundation for meaningful fellowship and unity is correspondingly undermined. Where there has been and continues to be fragmentation among God's people, it is not uncommon to find one or other of these factors involved.

Seeing the completeness of God's saving revelation in the Bible is one necessary element in finding a balance in our quest for unity, but it is not the only element. Following on from what we have said about the need to distinguish between what is essential for salvation and what is not, we need to go on to explore what constitutes gospel truth and what does not.

Paul's handling of the tensions between Jewish and Gentile converts and their respective congregations at this point in the New Testament is both fascinating and helpful. In his epistle to the Galatians, in which he addresses a group of churches which contain a significant number of Gentile converts, he faces a situation where a certain group was insisting that all Christians in all the churches not only had to profess faith in Jesus Christ as evidence of their salvation, but had also to adhere to a complete raft of requirements from Old Testament ceremonial law. Males were expected to receive the rite of circumcision, all were to observe the holy days of the Jewish calendar and respect the dietary restrictions which were set out in Mosaic law. The effect on Gentile converts in these churches was quite disturbing, not just in the sense that these observances belonged to an alien culture, but more significantly that they constituted an alien gospel. Paul almost seems to lose a grip on himself as he berates those who preach a gospel which either adds to or subtracts from the one which was entrusted to him by Jesus Christ and which, when proclaimed, led to the conversion of so many in Galatia and the formation of the churches to which he was now writing. He calls down a divine anathema on any who would dare to preach 'another gospel' (Gal. 1:6-9).

The point Paul is making is that there is an essential simplicity to the gospel which brings salvation, a simplicity which safeguards the two concerns we have already expressed, namely the sufficiency of Scripture and the distinction between what is primary and secondary. That is, all that is required for salvation and a place in the church is unadorned faith in Jesus Christ as Saviour and Lord as he is presented in the Scriptures. That essential simplicity of the gospel was encapsulated by the Reformers in the sixteenth century in their four great slogans: 'Scripture alone', 'Grace alone', 'Faith alone' and 'Christ alone'. The simplicity and the centrality of these gospel truths allowed the Reformers and their respective churches (as well as their successors) to exhibit and cultivate a remarkable spirit of catholicity in ecclesiastical fellowship – a degree of catholicity which is sadly lacking among many who claim to be their heirs in the present day.

There can be no mistaking the central truths which undergird the salvation of God's people: the uniqueness of Christ, the sufficiency of Christ and the faithfulness of Christ as he is revealed in God's holy Word. Where there is a genuine acknowledgement of those truths, then there is at least the beginning of a basis for fellowship and unity.

A Biblical Approach

The Bible not only puts a constraint on what we believe as the basis for our fellowship in Christ, it also constrains the way we hold our own convictions and respond to those with whom we may have differences. There is not only a 'what' in evangelical unity, but also a 'how'. One illuminating illustration is found in the testimony of a husband–wife team which made a lasting impression on those who knew them, but especially upon the apostle Paul who became their special friend.

Priscilla and Aquila were the couple in question and they are mentioned in several places in the book of Acts and in Paul's letters. (The fact that their names are always recorded in the unusual sequence of naming the wife first may well suggest that there were certain qualities that this woman possessed that simply made her stand out at the very remembrance of the pair.) The particular episode in which they are mentioned and which has a clear bearing on the way Christians are meant to relate to each other within the confines and constraints of God's Word involved one of the most notable preachers of New Testament times, a man called Apollos.

We first hear of this man and his gifts when he arrived in Ephesus (Acts 18:24-28). He was of Jewish extraction and was well versed in Old Testament Scripture. He was also renowned for his eloquence and his passion as a preacher. As soon as he came to Ephesus he immediately began to make a mark on that community through his ministry. It soon became apparent, however, to those who were already believers in that city that he had an inadequate understanding of baptism, only being familiar with the baptism of John and not that which had been commanded by Jesus himself. The response of Priscilla and Aquila to this deficiency was not to spread their discontent behind his back and undermine his ministry, or even to stand up and oppose him publicly on this point of doctrine. Rather we are told, 'they took him aside and explained to him the way of God more accurately' (Acts 18:26). With tact, love and gentleness they took him – possibly into their own home – and worked this matter through.

The contrast between their behaviour and what is so often the norm in many evangelical circles could not be more stark. Too many professing Christians seem to specialize in the dark art of character assassination in their dealings with others with whom they differ. The very fact that they can operate with apparent ease on the basis of

second-hand information says something about the way
they pursue relationships within the family of God. There
is no real effort to establish precisely what a person believes,
or to clear up any possible misunderstandings before
launching a verbal or written broadside against a fellow-
member of the body of Christ. If the spirit of this godly
couple were to be revived in so many of our churches today,
it would have a dramatic and constructive impact, not just
on the internal dynamics of congregational life and the unity
experienced there, but also on the dynamics of inter-church
fellowship and the wider calling we have in the Body of
Christ to ensure that as churches we are building one
another up as opposed to tearing one another down.

Ultimately it means emulating the spirit of Christ himself
who was not in the business of breaking imperfect reeds or
stifling wicks that were not burning with sufficient
brightness (Matt. 12:20). What we believe must of necessity
have an impact upon the way we hold our beliefs. That in
itself can be as much a test of orthodoxy as the theological
precision for which we instinctively look. A well-known
preacher and lecturer warning about the threats posed to
the future of Reformed Christianity from a human
perspective made the following observation. 'The
Reformed faith has a tendency to attract people who are
small-minded, socially inept, spiritual pygmies who latch
on to its theology as a cudgel with which they can beat
other people.' Such an analysis is chillingly accurate and
has been the painful experience of many churches which
have been disrupted through the influence of such people.
On a larger scale, that approach to truth has done untold
damage to the credibility of the gospel and the unity of the
church as a whole.

The Controlling Influence

The prominence of Scripture in the quest for unity among God's people cannot be over-emphasized. To marginalize it in any way is to leave the church attempting to erect man-made structures of fellowship which have no inherent strength or durability. To give God's Word the place it both demands and deserves in our fellowship within the church will allow it, in its own unique and powerful way, to break us out of conformity to the broken mould of a fallen and fractured humanity and transform us as our minds (and hearts) are renewed into a new corporate identity and relationship in Christ (Rom. 12:1-2). In that we shall not only be redefined in terms of what we are, but also remoulded in terms of how we live as 'Christ is formed' in us (Gal. 4:19) collectively and his Spirit truly governs the relationships that are forged through union and communion with Christ.

Chapter Five

Living Stones Built Together
The Raw Materials

The business of construction has become less of an art and more of a science in this technological era, not only in terms of design and planning, but particularly in the physical workmanship. The consequence all too often has been a style of building which is bland and utilitarian. From the vast inner-city commercial buildings to sprawling housing developments with oceans of identical homes, the price of efficiency and low-cost building has been the sacrifice of beauty, quality and detail. The signature of craftsmanship which seems to ooze from the stones of even the simplest of older buildings is just not there in so much of today's construction work.

A craft as simple as dry-stone walling is an art-form. It requires a most unusual skill to be able to select completely irregular rocks and stones and fit them together – without cement or binding material – with such precision and balance that the result is walling which is not only pleasing to the eye, but which is also incredibly resilient to the elements and to the ravages of time. The same kind of skills are evident also in a whole range of buildings from cottages to castles which were erected using undressed stone. In them also there is that combination of beauty and strength which makes them more than attractive relics of the past, but truly desirable properties for those who can afford them today. In terms of workmanship, they graphically enshrine the attractiveness of unity within diversity as an axiom of meaning and purpose within the universe.

Another aspect of the work of these master-builders of a bygone era is seen in the art of stone-dressing. The skilled masons who laboured on the Egyptian pyramids, for example, continue to astound historians of architecture and engineering over how, in a non-mechanized age, they managed to work with such enormous blocks of stone, trimming them with minuscule precision, transporting them to their site, hauling them up into position and fitting them together into elegant and enduring monuments to their craft. They too began with diverse and irregular materials, but in a different way were able to fashion them into one.

Similar and equally astounding skills were employed by those who worked on Solomon's temple. In the account of its construction we learn of stones cut and dressed in their quarries, transported to Jerusalem and set in place with a religious solemnity that reflected the unique and God-honouring purpose for which this building was destined. The entire construction itself was an architectural work of art, but all of it was consecrated to bringing glory to the God for whom it was erected. It was not intended to be an object of worship in itself, but rather a reflection of the glory of the God whose symbolic residence it was intended to be.

It was the memory of that temple which was not only to live on in the minds of the Jewish people, but which was to become a powerful emblem of God's eternal purpose in his work of building the church through his Son and preparing something which would truly reflect his glory and endure for ever.

It was the imagery of this temple that was picked up, first of all by Jesus with reference to what he would accomplish in redemption and how he would accomplish it (John 2:19), then by Paul with reference to the church as the temple-residence of the Holy Spirit and then by Peter as he develops the image to show how the church as the people of God is being made into the new and true temple for his glory. As we explore this imagery, it helps us to grasp something of the spiritual craftsmanship at work in the salvation and transformation of the church.

Diversity of Materials

In his first general epistle, Peter is addressing himself to an ever-diversifying range of people. The early church which he himself had been instrumental in bringing into existence in Jerusalem, had been a fairly homogenous grouping, in one sense. Even though the first converts on the Day of Pentecost and in the weeks that followed were from different ethnic backgrounds, the fact that they were either Jews or Proselytes gave them something in common which enabled them to identify with each other from the outset (although that in itself was no guaranteed safeguard against internal friction, as the dispute between Greek and Hebrew converts in Acts 6:1 was soon to prove). The scene changed radically, however, in a matter of decades. Those who had come to Jerusalem from different parts of the world for that memorable Feast of Pentecost and had been converted, went back to their homelands and were the means of seeing others converted and new churches established. Through that and, more directly, through the instigation of the Holy Spirit in the ministry of Paul, the gospel began to spread directly into Gentile territory and

people with no links with Judaism were becoming
Christians and were founding new congregations
throughout the Roman Empire. The church in the widest
sense was taking on the appearance of a kaleidoscope. It
was not long before the challenges of that diversity were
beginning to emerge, as we have seen already, in the
interaction between Christianity with a Jewish flavour on
the one hand and that which had emerged from paganism
on the other.

Other developments were to make the situation even
more complex, persecution being the most significant of
them all. When the Jewish authorities began to step up
their efforts to eradicate, or at least contain, the church,
numerous Christians were forced to flee (Acts 8:1). They
were literally scattered to the four winds and found
themselves having to settle in new and unfamiliar
surroundings among people who were complete strangers
in every way. This phenomenon was accelerated as the
Roman authorities began to exercise their powers in a
similar fashion. The overall effect of this was to create a
new *Diaspora* – a dispersion of God's people – in New
Testament times which was a mirror image of what had
been their experience in the Old Testament.

It was to these believers, scattered among the nations,
that Peter had pastoral concerns to express (1 Pet. 1:1).
Diversity was written all over their lives. They were diverse
individuals living in diverse countries among diverse
peoples and cultures. They seemed on the face of it to be a
motley crew who had nothing to hold them together. Yet
they did have a very real cohesive power that would
transform the way they looked at their circumstances and
the kind of outlook they had for the future, and it was to

this that Peter sought to point them.

As he speaks of what they are he immediately recognises their uniqueness and individuality. He calls them 'living stones' on God's building site (1 Pet. 2:5). For those, who through their Jewish background were already familiar with the Old Testament, he conjures up the scene of the construction of the temple in Jerusalem. What initially appears to be a scene of chaos and disorder – stones and rocks scattered in varying states of preparation – will eventually be transformed into something solid and compacted together. The sheer wonder and final beauty of it all only being emphasized by the unruly uniqueness of each component part in these early stages.

And so it was with the raw materials of God's new temple which were scattered over a site which encompassed the known world at that time. What could so easily have been viewed in terms of depressing imperfection in its present state, was meant to be seen in terms of its thrilling potential for its future state. The very fact that God was working with people from such differing ethnic and cultural backgrounds, the fact that he had stripped so many of these 'stones' down through displacement from homes and families, his decision to use a preponderance of people who were nothing and had nothing in themselves, all went into the miracle of what God was doing. He was bringing true unity out of unmistakable diversity and doing it in such a way as to bring all the glory and honour to himself in the process.

The timeless significance of all this for the church of all ages (regardless of the presence or absence of persecution) can be seen at two levels. In the context of the local congregation, the diversity of the body should be a cause

for celebration and not dismay. Some church leaders seem
to want to produce congregations of spiritual clones, but
God intends his churches to be gatherings of multicoloured
beauty. Although it runs completely counter to the
philosophy of contemporary church-growth gurus, Christ
never meant his followers to target homogenous units of
society – on the basis of class, colour, culture, or whatever
– and engineer them into churches. He told them to go
everywhere and do his work among all. The diversity
among Christians, which can all too easily be misconstrued
as a threat to harmony and fellowship, is really intended to
be an asset which proves that it is genuine. There is a real
sense in which a church in a given locality should reflect
the cross-section of the social, cultural and ethnic make-
up of its neighbourhood. It should be living proof that the
work of the gospel is to produce God's new society right
in the midst of a fallen one.

The other level at which this truth must have a bearing
is in the diversity between churches as well as within them.
The reality and wonder of this is becoming increasingly
self-evident in our age of a shrinking world. It is not all
that long since what was happening in other churches in
other parts of the world (and even other parts of our own
country) seemed quite remote. Perhaps a few slides from
missionaries, or the occasional visit while on holiday,
allowed for some sense of the church elsewhere being
different from the church of our immediate experience.
However, the ease of travel and the impact of mass
communication now means that even congregations in
remote villages in the Highlands of Scotland are being
exposed to Afro-Caribbean, Asian and even Glaswegian
forms of congregational life and worship. Conversely, those

used to the quiet life of the foothills of the Himalayas suffer the crass intrusions of western living.

Although the initial effect of such exposure can be quite disturbing for Christians who have never experienced church life beyond the immediate confines of their own fellowship or grouping, it must ultimately lead us to an even deeper and adoring appreciation of what God is doing among his people.

Imperfect Materials

The fact that there is such diversity in the raw materials God uses in the building of the church is not the only wonder: it is the fact that they are such imperfect materials. In a most amazing way he uses people whose lives are flawed. The 'living stones' of whom Peter is speaking, the raw materials for God's work, are stones contaminated by malice, deceit, hypocrisy, envy and slander (1 Pet. 2:1) – hardly the most appropriate materials for such an auspicious construction! Yet these are precisely the kind of raw materials God puts to use for this end.

This is true first of all at the point of incorporation into the family of God. When a person is received into fellowship with God and with his church, it is not because he or she is perfect, or in any sense naturally fit for such a holy communion. Quite the opposite: they are sinners, just like every other human being in the world. The significant difference being that they are justified sinners – people whose sins have been forgiven through the Lord Jesus Christ. The apostle Paul highlights the breathtaking wonder of that fact when he says,

> For while we were still helpless, at the right time Christ died for
> the ungodly. For one will hardly die for a righteous man; though
> perhaps for the good man someone would dare even to die. But
> God demonstrates His own love toward us, in that while we were
> yet sinners, Christ died for us (Rom. 5:6-8).

We must never allow ourselves to forget that we didn't
become part of the church of Jesus Christ because we were
in any sense 'good enough'. Perfection, our own merit,
was never the requirement for entry, rather the perfect
merits of the Saviour God sent for his people.

Similarly, it is not our perfection that qualifies us to
remain in the church let alone to serve in the church. It is
entirely on account of the grace of God that we continue to
enjoy fellowship with him. John Newton was quite right
when he penned the words, ''Tis grace has brought me
safe thus far, and grace will lead me home.'

The implication of this is brought out repeatedly and
powerfully in a succession of letters to the churches in the
apostolic call for humility on the part of God's people. A
humility which is modelled for us in the apostles themselves
and found pre-eminently in Jesus Christ. Thus Paul entreats
the congregation at Philippi to 'Have this attitude ... which
was also in Christ Jesus ...' (Phil. 2:5) and goes on to point
them to the Saviour who is characterized by a self-effacing
humility (Phil. 2:5-11). Elsewhere the same apostle,
summing up the practical implications of the gospel,
enumerates the first specific application as being that no-
one should 'think more highly of himself than he ought to
think; but to think so as to have sound judgment' (Rom.
12:3). It is not without significance that he goes on to
develop that principle in the context of living together and
serving together in the church.

Our natural fallen instinct is to think that we are something in ourselves when in fact we are not. This attitude continues to pervade the church and to threaten the fellowship of God's people and their ability to serve God faithfully and effectively together. It only serves to magnify the wonder of God's grace that he perseveres with such undeserving sinners, and has committed himself to finishing in them and through them the good work which he has begun.

The Workmanship of God

It took master craftsmen to construct the beautiful edifice which became Solomon's temple, and Peter draws attention to the ultimate Master Craftsman who is making something out of the rubble of ruined lives.

Peter's approach in writing to the scattered believers of his day is not unlike that employed by Paul in his epistles. He places side by side the great gospel indicatives and the corresponding great imperatives. He points first of all to what God has done, is doing and intends to do and then highlights the response these things require from those who truly believe.

He makes it clear that what is happening in their lives individually and collectively does not owe its origin to them as fallen human beings. It was not as though they decided to turn over a new leaf in life or that they resolved to work together with an agreed goal or focus in mind, rather that they had been caught up in something infinitely greater than themselves. 'And coming to Him [Jesus] ... you are being built ...' (1 Pet. 2:4-5). It was not that they were building themselves, or building each other up, but rather they were being built. They were not the agents in the exercise, but the materials which were being used.

Doubtless such a thought was unspeakably reassuring
for this early Christian community. It is clear from the time
of writing (probably in the early sixties AD) that the church
was beginning to feel the full force of opposition from
hostile forces. Initially the church had been spared much
serious persecution, certainly from the Roman authorities,
and had experienced significant internal encouragement
and cohesion, but now the situation was changing rapidly.
By the time of the Emperor Nero, the full force of imperial
might was beginning to turn against the church and that,
coupled with internal difficulties over conflicts, heresy and
apostasy, was fast undermining confidence. Thus, they
could not have had a more timely reminder that the present
(quite apart from the future) was in higher hands.

Indeed it has been a constant need of the church
throughout the ages to be brought back again and again to
the sovereign hand of God upon its life. It is only the solemn
word and promise of the Saviour that *he* will build his
church and not permit the gates of hell to prevail against it
(Matt. 16:18), that has actually preserved the church in the
world and guaranteed its future. The temptation for every
generation in the church has been to assume that there are
other things which undergird that security, however
commendable and vital, but it is ultimately Christ who is
our guarantee. The practical implication of that must be
for the church of all ages to respond in faith and obedience
to him and to his word.

The very fact that Peter tells these faltering
congregations that they are 'being built ...' (as opposed to
speaking either in the past tense, or the future) was another
significant element in what he wished to convey to them,

namely that God was in the process of doing something in them and through them which was not yet complete.

A preacher once told the story of a man who had heard of the workmanship of a master potter and was keen to acquire some of his pottery for himself. He went to the address he had been given, only to be confronted with a scene of apparent chaos and devastation. The potter himself was nowhere to be seen, but as the man's eye surveyed the tables and benches littered with tools, wheels, pots in various stages of completion and lumps of clay in its raw state, he caught sight of a notice which read,

> Please be patient
> He has not finished with us yet
> The showroom is upstairs!

The point of the illustration is self-evident! There can hardly be a better way of coming to terms with the obvious imperfection of both the church and believers on this side of heaven. As we have already seen, when a person is born again, God, by his Holy Spirit, has begun a new work in their life, but it is not brought to completion in that same instant. The finished product will not be seen until Jesus has returned and there is what he calls 'the renewal of all things' (Matt. 19:28). Until then, God's people need to be patient until his work of transformation is finally complete.

A significant element of that patience must involve being able to cope with imperfect lives in imperfect churches. Without for a moment condoning such imperfection, or feeling that nothing can be done about it, there needs to be a willingness to face the fact that in this world there will never be perfection – either in ourselves or others – so we must never lose heart because of that. The horizon to which we are working is not that of time, but of eternity.

The link between the horizons of time and eternity is to be found in Jesus Christ. The fact that Peter describes him as 'the living Stone' (1 Pet. 2:4) is a very graphic way of showing how all that God's people are and all they will finally be is contingent upon Jesus. In the same way as a building rests upon its foundation, so the people of God rest upon Christ as their cornerstone; if he is dislodged in any way, the entire edifice collapses.

It can be no accident that the apostle who was given the name Peter, or 'Rock', by Jesus (John 1:42), should latch on to that very terminology to explain not just the change that had come over his own life, but that which had become the experience of every child of God. All Christians are 'like living stones' (1 Pet. 2:5) who derive their new life from '*the* living Stone', that is Jesus. Indeed, the expression Peter uses to describe Jesus in this way has a built-in ambiguity in itself. It not only describes Jesus in the most unusual sense of being a stone which *has* life, but also describes him as the stone which *imparts* life.

If the language of stones and buildings is intended to convey (as surely it must) the sense of stability and durability, then this derives first and foremost from a shared life. It is because Jesus imparts his life through his Spirit to those who by nature are spiritually dead that they have any standing to begin with. It is that life from above which uniquely equips us for life in the fallen world below, a world where we live in the very atmosphere of death. But there is more to what Peter is saying.

The fact that Jesus is also the cornerstone of the church as a spiritual building guarantees that it will be able to survive all that would destabilize or demolish it. We have already spoken in an earlier chapter of the way in which Jesus Christ forms the foundation of his church in an objective sense. All he has accomplished in redemption has secured once and for all the salvation of his church. After he had passed through the nadir of his sufferings he would cry to his Father, 'It is finished' (John 19:30)! There was nothing left to do, there was nothing left to accomplish; the salvation of all of God's people for the entirety of history had been secured. The church can never afford to lose sight of that great objective reality as the very basis of her existence. However, there is another sense in which she needs to come to Christ as cornerstone for the day-to-day experience of that salvation.

Despite the settled nature of Christ's foundational work, the subjective outworking of that in the corporate experience of the life of the church is a very different thing. The contrast between these two elements of life in the church is well captured by Samuel John Stone in his great hymn about the church:

> The church's one foundation
> Is Jesus Christ her Lord;
> She is his new creation
> By water and the Word;
> From heaven he came and sought her
> To be his holy bride;
> With his own blood he bought her,
> And for her life he died ...
>
> ... Though with a scornful wonder
> Men see her sore oppressed,
> By schisms rent asunder,
> By heresies distressed,

Yet saints their watch are keeping,
Their cry goes up, 'How long?'
And soon the night of weeping
Shall be the morn of song.

Mid toil and tribulation,
And tumult of her war,
She waits the consummation
Of peace for evermore;
Till with the vision glorious,
Her longing eyes are blest,
And the great church victorious,
Shall be the church at rest.

Although in this world it is true to say that the church is
'victorious' – she shares in the victory Christ secured on
her behalf at Calvary – it will not be until in the world to
come that she can truly be 'the church at rest'.

The only way, then, that imperfect Christians in
imperfect churches can retain their sanity and enjoy any
kind of stability in a most imperfect world is through
actually resting in an ongoing sense upon the One who is
their cornerstone. Thus, as Peter was addressing believers
in a turbulent world, he was directing them to the Christ
upon whom they were built but also in whom they would
find their daily rest. It was the same Jesus who had calmed
the storms of nature, silenced the uproar of demons and
who had said so pointedly, 'Come to Me ... and I will give
you rest ...' (Matt. 11:28-30). As we rest in him by faith
and communion on a daily basis, we have the wherewithal
to cope with our present imperfections and the
inextinguishable assurance that we shall soon enjoy an
everlasting rest.

The End Product

One of the greatest encouragements and incentives given to the church in its imperfect state is the glorious prospect of what she shall be in her final state. Paul speaks of her as the Bride of Christ, finally free from any and all blemishes, presented to Christ and for Christ for an eternity of bliss (Eph. 5:27). That same vision of a glorified church is one of the last sights we see as God's great self-revelation comes to its end. John is allowed to see the New Jerusalem coming down out of heaven like a bride adorned for her husband (Rev. 21:2).

Once more, the original context of that vision and revelation could hardly have been more pertinent. The church in those latter days of the ageing apostle seemed to be anything but a renewed community or anything like a bride bedecked in all her finery. She was seemingly in tatters, having suffered the ravages of persecution and deprivation, coupled with the internal strife which had done and was continuing to do so much damage to her welfare and witness. Already in his prophecy, John has had to act as Christ's legal agent bringing news of his displeasure and judgement to a number of these very congregations, so where on earth was there hope for the future?

The hope and encouragement come from the same Saviour who is seen at the beginning of Revelation standing among the seven golden lamp-stands which represent the church (Rev. 1:13). No matter how severe the opposition, no matter how painful the disruption, here is the Christ who has pledged himself to his people for eternity by everlasting covenant and he will not leave his work in them unfinished.

In the midst of present difficulties the people of God

can become myopic – short-sighted – and obsessed with
the immediate state of affairs. Our eyes must ever focus,
not on what we are, but ultimately what we shall be in
Christ!

Chapter Six

'That They May be One'
The Highest Aspiration

So far we have been attempting to set out the elements which are essential to an understanding of true Christian unity – a unity which is evangelical in the fullest possible sense. It is something which is patterned on the godhead itself, mirroring the unity-in-diversity which is integral to the glory of God in heaven which the redeemed humanity is to reflect on earth. By God's holy revelation alone can we understand what this involves, in principle and in practice. Thus the quest for unity among the people of God can never be divorced from the Scriptures and their power to both inform and transform those who are exposed to them. The route-map through the minefield of fragmentation is set out for us in the Bible and points us to the ultimate reconciliation that will be experienced fully in heaven. We have seen too that there is a great need for healthy realism in our entire approach to this thorny problem, appreciating how much we need to understand ourselves, first of all in our fallen state before conversion, but then also in the present state of imperfection after conversion. Only in glory will we actually experience perfect unity, and so long as we remain on the earth we must face the responsibility of working out God's perfect salvation in a very imperfect world.

When we are aware of the elements involved in

establishing meaningful unity among the people of God on earth, we can go on to consider more fully the mechanics and dynamics of how they work together in practice. What God has established in grace must translate into what his people experience in life and in the fellowship of his church in the world.

This brings us inevitably into the realm of the great biblical mystery of divine sovereignty and human responsibility. There is a perceived tension between the domain of God and the domain of man in the full outworking of redemption. Attempts are often made to resolve the tension by emphasizing one party in the relationship at the expense of the other and it is perhaps because of this that Christian experience ends up being impoverished and the worship of God devalued. There is no straightforward resolution of this tension in terms of human logic, but there is a resolution in the realm of faith and experience. Our minds may not be able to grasp fully *how* it works, but there can be no doubting or denying that it does work.

It is to that experience in the corporate life of the church that we now want to turn our attention. We need to consider the practicalities of applying the truths and principles already outlined into action.

The starting point in this must surely be at the level of aspiration. How we live and what we do is profoundly affected by what we aspire to, not just in life in general, but in Christian living in particular. This is true in the spiritual realm in a way that involves not just our private and personal hopes and desires, but also those of God our Saviour. If we go back to our building site for a moment we can perhaps appreciate what we mean by this. The day-to-day problems which arise on most construction sites are due most often to a conflict between the aspirations of the architect and those of the builder. The architect has a very clear idea of what he wants and the most appropriate way of getting there, but at many points the builder will see things quite differently and perhaps even decide to take matters into his own hands, with inevitable consequences.

The inevitable consequences of such conflict of aspiration on God's building site in the corporate life of his people is not hard to see. We too are prone to taking matters into our own hands with regard to our sanctification, personally and corporately. That is bound to have an effect on our relationship with God on the one hand, but also on relationships within the church on the other. Even though it may be true in earthly terms that builders at times know better than architects, it is never true to say that the church knows better than God. Thus our constant need is to see what God desires and subordinate our own desires and aspirations to his.

The Highest Aspiration of Christ

We can never underestimate the importance of prayer in Scripture as one of God's means of bringing us into a richer and deeper experience of himself and his great salvation. That is true in terms of its being a means to an end. It is, if you like, the spiritual umbilical cord which links the child of God by the Spirit of God to the experience of fellowship with God. We were never meant for independent existence, isolated from God our Maker. Thus prayer is the conscious expression of our dependence upon him for all things. It is also true, however, in the sense that it provides an amazing insight into the concerns of the soul that prays.

In the Old Testament we have glimpses into the prayers of God's great leaders like Nehemiah (Neh. 1:5-11) and Daniel (Dan. 9:4-19) in such a way as to show us God's great purpose through them for his people. The same is true in an unmistakable way in the prayers of the apostle Paul which are integral to his letters. Indeed it is often true to say that understanding his prayers is to understand the purpose of his writing in each particular situation. They show us not merely Paul's, but God's concerns for his people in those churches and through all time.

It should not surprise us then that the recorded prayers of Jesus should allow us a glimpse into some of the greatest concerns that God has for his people. (The very fact that Jesus *prays* for these concerns, as opposed to simply decreeing their fulfilment, says something about the mystery of how these ends are realized, as we have already indicated above.) Recognizing the aspirations of the Saviour at the heart of his prayers is to identify the highest aspirations the church can have for herself.

It is striking to note that the longest recorded prayer of Jesus is one that dwells much on the need for oneness among his people. The setting is the eve of his arrest and crucifixion. He has spent the evening in discourse with his disciples in the Upper Room, explaining, in the fullest detail they have thus far heard, what was about to happen to him, what it would mean and what they could subsequently expect. Then he galvanizes the entirety of that evening's instruction with a prayer that was to be etched in the memories of the disciples for the remainder of their lives and stamped on the collective consciousness of the church for all time.

Many concerns pressed in upon the Saviour at that

moment in his experience, not least the enormity of the ordeal which would lead to such crisis in prayer in Gethsemane and which required the aid and support of an angel from heaven during those dark hours. It is almost incredible to think that Christ should be so taken up with his concern for the unity of his people at this point. We might well have expected him to cry out for sustaining grace for himself, or for understanding minds for his followers, but instead his burden is for his family and the preservation of the bond which unites it.

The prominence of this concern under such circumstances must surely serve as a rebuke to prayers of so many of the Lord's people for whom the burden for their fellowship is all but absent and barely features in the public expression of their prayers in and for the church. The scale of priorities which governed the prayers of the Redeemer have to be the best pattern for the priorities in the prayers of the redeemed.

Having prayed for himself in the face of the impending ordeal of Calvary, he goes on to commend the apostolic band to the Father, knowing that he is soon to depart from them. He prays for their protection (John 17:11), the goal of that protection being, 'that they may be one, even as We are'. Then, having prayed for the disciples, he goes on to pray for those who would believe in him through their message. At this point (as the body of believers must inevitably further diversify) his prayer becomes even more pointed in its concern for unity:

'I do not ask on behalf of these alone, but for those also who believe in Me through their word; that they may all be one; even as You, Father, are in Me, and I in You, that they also may be in Us; that

the world may believe that You sent Me. The glory which You
have given Me I have given to them, that they may be one, just as
We are one; I in them and You in Me, that they may be perfected
in unity, so that the world may know that You sent Me, and loved
them, even as You have loved Me' (John 17:20-23).

We will take time in the next chapter to look more
closely at what lies behind this extraordinary request of
Jesus at this critical juncture in his mission and ministry,
but at this point we want to concentrate on the nature of
the unity for which he prays.

In the first place it is unity which is bound up with the
divine protection, a protection which guarantees that the
little flock will not fragment. (The fact that Judas is clearly
marked out as being a special case bound up with the
mystery of God's will [John 17:12], shows that his removal
from the fellowship of that little congregation did not impair
God's ultimate purpose to redeem it as a body.) Thus the
saving, keeping power of God in salvation has to do not
just with individual perseverance in the faith, but corporate
faithfulness; a faithfulness which not only preserves the
vertical relationship of communion with God, but also
horizontal communion of faithfulness to the body and to
each of its members.

God's new creation – with its focus on the church as his
redeemed and renewed community – is in need of his
special protection from the same enemy whose design was
to disrupt and destroy the unified beauty of creation in its
perfect state. Thus the grief that we feel in reaction to the
disrupted world in which we live should be felt even more
strongly when we see the fellowship of God's people
fractured through our own sins and failures. It is nothing

less than a Satanic attempt to assault God through an assault on his workmanship.

In the second place (and in a way which follows logically from the first point) we need to appreciate how much the glory of God is bound up with the unity of his people (John 17:22). When the latter is impaired, the former is obscured.

As the ultimate focus of Christ's prayer was the supreme glory of the Godhead, it is a humbling thing to see the way it is linked to such an apparently inglorious body as the church and especially to that particular facet of church life at which it is at its most vulnerable. Yet that is where the focus of God's glory is most visible in our fallen and fragmented world. What has been disrupted through sin has been restored and put right in salvation – that is the ultimate glory of the gospel. The final outcome of Christ's work of redemption is not merely the deliverance of a disparate array of isolated individuals, but instead the new and unified people of God. The old fragmented race in sin will be replaced by the new and reunited humanity in grace. Nothing could be more integral to all that is bound up with the glory of God as a total entity as opposed to the individual facets of glory. Practically all of those glorious facets converge in what the saving grace of God in Christ has accomplished, namely the creation of the church.

The impact of this prayer (as much as its God-given outcome) is to be seen in quite a striking fashion in the later writings of two of the disciples who were least disposed to providing a unifying influence within the apostolic fellowship: John – whose explosive temperament is manifest in his nick-name, 'Son of Thunder' – and Peter, renowned for his ability to incite and upset even the best of company. Yet both of these men demonstrate a concern for the preservation of the unity of brethren that can only be traced back to what they heard their Master pray on that memorable night in the upper-room in Jerusalem.

Peter's first epistle in particular contains a noteworthy array of exhortations to heartfelt love (1:22), transparent relationships (2:1), unified building work (2:5), a spirit of submission (2:13), marital devotion (3:1), harmony (3:8), hospitality (4:9) and humility (5:6). All of these traits and those he relates to them are the essential ingredients to sustaining harmonious fellowship within the church. So, too, John homes in upon love for our brothers in Christ as the touchstone of our being in Christ (1 John 2:10-11). In the advancing years of New Testament Christianity – when so many internal and external pressures on the church were manifesting themselves in the fracture-lines appearing in the fellowship of the saints – both of these shepherd-elders saw the pressing need to hold together what Satan was conspiring to blow apart.

In the midst of their own trials at that time they had been captivated by that overriding aspiration of Christ on the threshold of his own ultimate trial that the outcome of it all would be the impregnable unity of his flock. As an essential element of that 'joy' which was set before him as the consequence of Calvary (Heb. 12:2), the unity of his redeemed people was something to be prized and cherished by those who would come to experience it by his grace and to be kept as the great goal of the corporate life of faith.

Shared Aspiration

It should go without saying that what Christ desires, his people also should desire. Thus his aspirations for his church should become the church's aspiration for herself. The importance he attaches to something should govern the degree of importance his people attach to it.

As we have seen already, the issue of unity among God's people lies so much at the heart of Christ's concern and purpose that those who genuinely know and love him are simply not allowed to relegate it on the scale of their priorities, either in prayer or in practice.

Indeed, it is a measure of the extent to which a church possesses the mind and Spirit of Christ to see how much it prizes its oneness and labours to preserve it. The great High Priestly prayer of Christ should be embedded in the deepest desires of all his people.

Having said that, when a church begins to take seriously what Christ is seeking in this prayer, it will inevitably encounter the difficulties set in the way of its being realized in the experience of his people. Obstacles begin to present themselves from the very outset.

A Twisted Aspiration

Sadly, the most damaging obstacles to progress towards the goal of fellowship and unity in the church arise from within. They start when the aspirations given to the church by her Saviour are taken and twisted by his people.

The goals of Christian living are ones which Christ gives us through his Word. They are invariably high and lofty goals which are beyond the reach of natural human ability and even, at times, beyond the scope of our fallen, finite understanding. When confronted with such goals and the

struggle they create in trying to cope with them, the
temptation is strong to try to mould them into a more
manageable form.

An obvious example of such manipulation is seen in
the Bible's teaching on sanctification. Jesus says,
'Therefore you are to be perfect, as your heavenly Father
is perfect' (Matt. 5:48) – strong language with strong
implications. How are Christians to reconcile such a high
goal with the squalid reality of repeatedly falling short of
God's standard of righteousness in the life of faith? The
solution for some has been to develop a theology of
perfectionism which hinges on redefining the doctrine of
sin. The goal-posts are moved in order to remove the
discomfort of God's demands upon our lives as his people.
Aspirations are simply twisted into a shape which is more
palatable.

The same kind of treatment has been meted out to the
concerns Jesus lays before his people as well as before
God in this great High Priestly prayer. This has happened
in a number of ways.

If we take seriously the language that Jesus uses in this
prayer, it is impossible to escape the force of his requests
and the expectation of how their answer will have a radical
effect on the life of his church. Couple this with the fact
that the prayers of Jesus simply cannot go unanswered and
we are left struggling to see where that answer is to be
found in the fellowship of the saints.

Some have come to understand the unity for which he
prays in purely spiritual terms. Focusing on the fact that
the unity for which Christ prays is to mirror the unity which
exists within the Godhead (John 17:11, 21-23), it is argued
that this is essentially a spiritual unity which simply exists.

This is tied in with Paul's description of the unity of believers as being '... of the Spirit, in the bond of peace' (Eph. 4:3). What is envisaged is simply a bond which *de facto* unites the church universal by virtue of its union with Christ through his Spirit. It is a unity over which we have no control, it is the sovereign gift of God to his people. It is more evident at some times than at others, but regardless of how manifest it may be, it is always there as a constant.

Such a view of Christian unity is attractive because it preserves the integrity of what Jesus prays for in this passage while removing the discomfort of seeing so little evidence of his prayer being answered in the life of the church in the world. However, its great weakness is the fact that Jesus makes it clear that it is a unity that will be seen, not merely by his redeemed people, but ultimately by a fallen, watching world (John 17:21, 23). We cannot wriggle out of our responsibility before God towards each other by simply spiritualizing what God requires in our corporate life together.

Others have sought to resolve the tension by an altogether different route. They genuinely wish to take at face value the force of Christ's prayer for a unity which is visible and they respond accordingly with a pursuit of unity purely in the realm of the visible. Such aspirations were the driving force behind the early decades of the *World Council of Churches*. Hence the emphasis in the quest for this unity was in organization and co-operation. Great schemes of unity were set in motion – not only in the *WCC*, but also in the main denominations of the world – which were hammered out in the chambers of committees and the floors of public debate. The belief was that it is possible to find a negotiated unity for the people of God, a form of words to which all could subscribe and within which all could agree.

The fundamental problem with this approach to the contents of this prayer of Jesus is the very fact that it is a *prayer*, not a programme! Its outcome is something which only God can impart and not even the best ecumenical diplomats and statesmen will ever be able to achieve it. It has taken almost eighty years of ecumenical aspiration, endeavour and failure to demonstrate that such an understanding of what it means for the people of God to be one has little to commend it and no future to look forward to.

If the church is truly to attain to the heights on earth for which her Saviour prayed, then she cannot afford to tamper with the very essence of those high aspirations, by simply manipulating them into a form that seems more acceptable to fallen minds.

Living with a Holy Tension

The most natural way to interpret the prayer for unity offered by Jesus on this solemn occasion is to see it as both spiritual *and* visible. Despite the fact that there are obvious tensions involved, this preserves the essence of what Jesus has in view and maintains the responsibility he lays upon the shoulders of his people to pursue, through the enabling of his Spirit, the goal which he himself has laid before them.

The end product will never be a perfect visible unity on earth, because the Bible never promises complete transformation of life for God's children in this world. Nevertheless, it will be a real unity. It will take full cognisance of our failure to measure up to the standards of fellowship God expects, it will never let go of his perfect ideal as the object of our corporate pursuits, but it will also eagerly appropriate God's great provision for us as we seek these ends. On the one hand there is the provision of pardon for all our failures. We will never cease to be thankful that there is forgiveness for us as we openly acknowledge that the schisms in which we are involved as the people of God both grieve and quench the Spirit of God. God will not hold us to ransom for failure in this area if we are truly penitent and confess our sins before him. More than that, we will gladly recognize our own deficiencies and inadequacies in our efforts to build fellowship among the saints and will welcome and rely upon the supernatural resources God places at our disposal in his sanctifying Spirit. As we draw upon his enabling grace and keep in step with his wise and perfect leading, we will achieve through him what we could never achieve on our own.

The Purpose of Redemption

As we take this approach to understanding what Jesus is seeking in prayer on the eve of his crucifixion – the very climax of his redemptive work – we find ourselves being drawn in to the very heart of God's plan of redemption itself. More than anything else, it will bring us to an understanding of the reality which surrounds us in the world and the glorious reality which is set before us in the gospel.

God's plan to save is set against the ugly backdrop of a world held in the grip of sin and its consequences. By its very nature, as we have already seen, the very essence of sin is to divide and fragment. When God warned Adam in the Garden of Eden that the consequence of disobedience would be death, it was in no sense a threat about the cessation of life, but rather that of separation and fragmentation. There would be the separation between God and man on earth as Adam and Eve were to suffer the immediate consequence of their sin which was spiritual death. Their fellowship with God was broken and in turn their fellowship as the embryonic human race was likewise fractured. This would in turn lead to the division of soul and body which comes in physical death and ultimately, for those who die without faith, the eternal separation of body and soul from God for ever in hell. Sin divides and fragments all that come within its control. The beauty of the gospel is that God's grace heals and restores all that come within his embrace through Jesus Christ!

God's goal in redemption is nothing short of a renewed and perfected community in a restored and perfected world and universe. It was that very purpose that Jesus was on the verge of sealing and securing as he prayed with the prospect of Calvary before him. As he focused on the outcome of what lay before him, he provides his believing people with the key to understanding what salvation is all about.

A Vision to Keep in View

If Christ encouraged himself with the vision of what lay beyond his great ordeal, how much more will that vision continue to encourage his people through all generations in the midst of their lesser ordeals as they grow in corporate grace.

It is always when God's people have lost sight of that great vision of unity, so much cherished by Christ, that the church has fallen prey to fragmentation in its many and various forms. It is striking and sobering to remember in the middle of friction and dispute between those who still recognize each other to be true Christians that they will one day have to share the same heaven. If that is the end of our journey in salvation, then there is no place for the apparent luxury of going our separate ways on earth. We do not resolve our differences in isolation from each other, but together in dependence upon God's promised grace and help. Together we will be humbled before God and before our brothers and sisters, acknowledging first our own guilt and failure before pointing it out in others, and never tiring of pursuing the very thing for which Jesus Christ our Saviour laid hold on us in the first place.

There can be no greater priority in the life of the church, because there was no greater concern in Christ's work of salvation. Maintaining that same vision and goal in the corporate life of the church – both within congregations and between congregations – will determine to a very large extent the spiritual health and welfare of the people of God and their corporate usefulness in their service in the world.

Chapter Seven

'That the World May See and Believe'
The Purpose

It is not hard to see why many, if not most, Christians find it hard to get excited about ecumenism and the issues which relate to true Christian unity. More often than not it becomes an end in itself. It gets wrapped up in self-perpetuating committees, endless streams of paper and becomes what amounts to the exercises of a spiritual mutual-appreciation society, but goes no further. They fail to see any ultimate purpose in it all.

Nothing will make churches sit up and take notice of the importance of this issue more than to recognize that there is an ultimate purpose in it all, one which Christ himself identifies for us. Far from being an abstract, or academic, matter which relates only to infra-church fellowship and inter-church politics, it impinges upon the very heart of the gospel itself. As we have noted already, the overriding concern as Jesus prays is that the church might be one so that the world may believe!

It follows then that there is an intimate relationship between the unity of God's people *in* the world and the proclamation of God's message *to* the world. A relationship which has implications running in a number of directions.

A Gospel Which is Seen as well as Heard

The primary thing (in human terms) which will make a fallen, rebel race take notice of God's message of salvation is the impact of his people's lives. The spread of that message is bound up, not just with what the church does and says, but what it is and how it lives. Thus, in Old Testament terms, the people of God in Israel were to be a light to the Gentiles (Isa. 49:6; 44:1ff.),[8] bearing witness to the one true God among the pagan nations of the world. God's honour and God's message were bound up with their life and conduct together as his people, thus when there was internal failure and fragmentation in Israel, it had repercussions for God and his glory in the eyes of a watching world.

Jesus picks up the same truth and applies it pointedly to the church when he says to his followers in the Sermon on the Mount, '*You* are the light of the world ...' (Matt. 5:14). Their calling in fellowship with Christ is to reflect the light which emanates from him, the One who is the Light of the world in the fullest sense. That calling is a collective calling for all God's people. The witness of their corporate life and testimony has the effect of bringing light into the darkness of a sinful world.

Thus, as the world is exposed to God's gospel, it will be struck not just by the wonder of what it says, but arguably even more so by the wonder of what it does. Here is something which changes lives and transforms the way in which people live and relate to one another. Indeed Jesus goes so far as to say that the way in which Christians relate to one another will be *the* distinguishing mark of their discipleship and the evidence of his saving grace: 'By this all men will know that you are My disciples, if you have love for one another' (John 13:35).

Although there is that sense in which the transforming power of God's grace will be manifest initially at a personal level – a life which is changed so that it begins to take on the shape and contours of Christ himself – it will be manifest most powerfully at the level of community. That takes us into a realm which is way beyond the scope of self-reformation or exceptions to the norm. When the world encounters a community of diverse people who are bound together in genuine love and devotion, it is brought face to face with Christ. The only explanation for such fellowship, whether seen in a local congregation, or in the way churches are able to relate to each other, is that God has done something in their lives through his Son. His gospel has done its work!

It is precisely this point that Jesus is making as he prays, 'that they may all be one ... so that the world may believe ...' The unity of his people in the world would reflect the glorious unity of the Godhead in heaven and endorse the reality of the gospel's power to save on the earth. God's message will not only be heard from heaven, but also seen in the world in the lives of his redeemed people. It will be seen as that which gets to the very heart of the world's deepest problem, providing God's antidote to the divisive and destructive power of sin.

This was to be made manifest in a remarkable way in the life of the New Testament church as it grew and established itself in the Roman world. As the apostles and early Christians took the gospel throughout the Roman Empire, it cut across all kinds of barriers: ethnic, cultural, intellectual, social, gender-related and others. In so doing it sent a worrying signal to those who held the reins of power in the Empire, leading to the report recorded in Acts:

'These who have turned the world upside down have come here too' (Acts 17:6, NKJV). What the imperial authorities had failed to accomplish by military and political means with their renowned *Pax Romana*, the followers of Jesus were accomplishing by spiritual means with unnerving effectiveness wherever they went. Regardless of how people may have responded, the gospel was being noticed.

The lesson in this for the church of all ages should hardly need emphasizing, yet it is exactly at this point that she has lost her way. The witness of local congregations, entire denominations and wider fellowships of churches – however orthodox they may be in their theology – has been impaired and sometimes even destroyed by the divisions within their ranks. The beauty of the gospel proclaimed from their pulpits has been tarnished and disgraced by the conduct of their lives. As Mahatma Gandhi rightly said, the church is her own worst enemy. Indeed, more serious than that, the greatest enemy of the gospel is all too often the professing people of the Christ of whom it speaks.

Unity Which is Visible as well as Theoretical

The argument that it is a *visible* unity for which Christ prays is at its sharpest at this point. It is impossible for the world to believe that God sent his Son to be its Saviour merely as a response to a notional or theoretical unity among his people. For them to respond meaningfully to the former, they must be able to witness the latter in a meaningful way. A spiritual unity which is acknowledged as a theological nicety, but which does not translate into practical reality, can never make the kind of impact on a fallen world that Jesus prays it will.

Jesus prays for something which will be both seen and

felt in the world and which will impact in a life-transforming way those who find themselves exposed to it through the life and witness of the church.

At the end of the day, the gospel involves more than subscribing to certain truths about Christ and God – even the devil himself is able to make such an ascription. It is not merely truth in itself to which Jesus is pointing, but rather truth as it impacts on the lives and relationships of those who are exposed to it. The outworking of the gospel actually draws people into all that it proclaims. Thus, as Jesus prays, 'that they may be one, *just as* We are one' (John 17:22), he is directing us to the fact that the bond that unites his people is a supernatural bond. Christian unity and fellowship involve more than simply copying, or mirroring, the unity of the Godhead; it requires the supernatural power of the Godhead to be at work in people's lives.

The power and effects of sin in our fallen, corporate nature as human beings are such that it takes nothing less than divine intervention to turn our lives around and recreate what the fall has destroyed. Jesus prays for such life-transforming power to be poured out from heaven upon his church.

As this happens visibly in the corporate life of the people of God, it not only draws attention to itself in the eyes of a watching world, it ultimately draws attention to God as the only source of such transforming grace. In so doing it will become a further instrument in his hand to elicit the response of faith from others who are destined to be part of his family.

As the church began to expand in those early days of New Testament church history, it was this extraordinary unifying power of the gospel which was so striking for all to see. The message of Christ and his power to save was able to cross every conceivable human barrier. As people were converted and added to the church, they were drawn in from all sorts of backgrounds. These included the wealthy and the poor, male and female, young and old, slave and free, educated and illiterate, Jews and Gentiles. Something was being established which had no earthly parallel. No human efforts to unite people had ever had such success either by political or coercive methods. This was something which stood alone in the history of human relationships.

The only explanation for what was being seen and experienced was that God himself was responsible, that this strange phenomenon was the result of supernatural intervention, bearing out the heart of the gospel – that in the Person of Jesus Christ, God had indeed sent his own Son into the world to bring salvation to his people (John 17:21). The end-product of his coming was to establish on earth a unity among men whose only parallel was the unity between the Persons of the Trinity in heaven.

It is only when such a unity – incredible as it may seem to human minds – moves beyond the level of theological and theoretical nicety to living reality, that it can serve to authenticate the gospel in the way Jesus has prayed.

A Witness Which is Concerned with Being as well as Doing
Such an understanding of what Jesus is saying in this prayer must have profound implications for our understanding of the church's witness in the world.

It is immediately apparent that Jesus is not talking about something which is programmatic, but, rather, which is personal. It must start with what we are in ourselves and in our relationships and not in what we might attempt to put in place through artificial structures of one sort or another. Only as God's saving grace begins to effect transformation in personal character and corporate relationships will this change endorse and authenticate the gospel and its witness. Indeed, that saving power will overflow quite naturally from the sphere of the redeemed community of the church into the wider community in which she has been placed and among which she labours in the gospel. The very testimony of what we are as the people of God – as individuals and as a community transformed by grace – will demonstrate as well as explain what is involved in this message of salvation through Christ which we proclaim. What the world sees in us will stimulate the kind of questions which allow us to give a reason for the hope that is within us (1 Pet. 3:15).

All too often that element of witness has been overlooked and neglected by the church. Its approach to witness and evangelism has erred on the side of being programmatic instead of personal. In so doing it has lost the most powerful, visible dynamic the gospel possesses: the living testimony to its saving power. The world can see through programmes of evangelism and sense whether or not this is a conscience-salving exercise on the part of the church or a genuine attempt to reach a lost and perishing world with the message of eternal life. If it is not the latter, any attempt to reach the world with the gospel is bound to run out of steam and come to nothing. Worse than that, it will discredit God's name and dishonour his message to the world.

It was that inconsistency of life and witness that lay at

the heart of Israel's spiritual decline in the Old Testament and its terminal ineffectiveness as God's light to the Gentiles. This was the concern which lay at the heart of Daniel's prayer as he interceded for the Israelites during their captivity. He identified himself fully with his people and with their sinful failures (even though he himself was innocent of their unfaithfulness) and reminded God that God's own honour was bound up with their conduct. He rounded off his memorable plea on their behalf with the words,

> So now, our God, listen to the prayer of Your servant and to his supplications, and for Your sake, O Lord, let Your face shine on Your desolate sanctuary. O my God, incline Your ear and hear! Open Your eyes and see our desolations and the city which is called by Your name; for we are not presenting our supplications before Your on account of any merits of our own, but on account of Your great compassion. O Lord, hear! O Lord, forgive! O Lord, listen and take action! For Your own sake, O my God, do not delay, because Your city and Your people are called by Your name (Dan. 9:17-19).

He was so conscious of the fact that the honour of God and the reputation of his people were so closely interwoven that he could not bear the disgrace being brought upon the Lord as a result of the sinful conduct of those who bore his name. Even though in a sense it was the name of Israel which had become a byword in the eyes of the nations, in reality it was the name of their God and the credibility of his message which was being dragged in the gutter.

The pertinence of that failure of Old Testament Israel and the passion of the prayer of this Old Testament saint speaks volumes to the church of all ages. As we have indicated in various ways already, the internal failures of the church, not just through her conduct, but perhaps especially through her internal relationships, have a dramatic bearing not just upon her own reputation, but ultimately upon God's reputation and the standing of his gospel before the watching world.

It puts the people of God on notice to be aware of the ramifications of their conduct. More than that, however, it must surely put a note of urgency into their prayers that they should be truly focused on all that will bring glory and honour to their Saviour God and not merely demand a response to an endless stream of requests that never seems to rise above the horizons of self-interest of one sort or another.

This is not to say that there will never be times when it is necessary to deal with differences within the family of God, however, when such differences do arise we will deal with them in a way which in itself proves that the church is different from the world. It will demonstrate that the dynamics of family life among the people of God are suffused with the same grace that is the source of their salvation.

The bottom line is that the witness of the church is intimately bound up with the behaviour of the church. That is true in terms of personal conduct; moral and spiritual hypocrisy will inevitably undermine any testimony to gospel grace that is supposed to change people's lives. But it equally applies to corporate conduct. A congregation which is divided within itself will have a hard time convincing any seeker that may come through its doors that the family of God has any more to offer than the family of a fallen race. Likewise, a church which cannot bring itself to relate in some meaningful way to other nearby churches which preach the same message (without necessarily being identical in their practices of church life and worship) cannot but impair the broader credibility of the gospel. At the end of the day, the gospel of our Lord Jesus Christ is not the private property of a few limited expressions of the church. It is the property of the Lord himself and wherever he is at work his voice will be heard and his people should not only acknowledge that, but should rejoice in it, too!

Gospel unity within the church will transcend all party lines. It will cross denominational boundaries as well as cultural ones. It will prove itself bigger than the pride and prejudice which all too often contaminate even the best of Christian relationships. It will stretch so far as to be able to rejoice even when the message of salvation through Christ seems to be preached in a spirit of rivalry – as was the case with Paul in what was happening around Philippi (Phil. 1:12-20).

Nothing should concentrate our minds more on the issues raised by God's call for unity among his people than the fact that the honour of God and the credibility of his message is at stake. It is not a matter of personal feelings or parochial distinctions, but the very heart of the gospel and the experience of salvation. Only when the church has established that critical horizon in her understanding of herself, her relationships and the task which God has entrusted to her, can she truly begin to bear testimony to the Lord before the world in a way which is God-honouring and life-transforming and which will display the full splendour of the gospel message.

Chapter Eight

'The Eye Cannot Say ...'
Hindrances from Within

Given all that we have said about the reality of spiritual unity within the family of God and the obligation laid upon every Christian to pursue that unity, it is only right that we give some thought to the obstacles which stand in the way of achieving its full enjoyment. There has never been a time in the life or experience of the church when the unity of the body has not been disrupted in some way or another. Even the best of relationships within the wider whole have all too often been impaired: Paul had a major disagreement with Barnabas which led to a parting of their ways (Acts 15:36-41); the two key figures in the revival years of the eighteenth century – George Whitefield and John Wesley – divided over doctrinal differences; and many others, perhaps with a lesser profile, stand with them in the messy, painful and embarrassing divisions which litter the path along which the pilgrim people of God have walked through the centuries. Over and above the breakdown at the level of inter-personal relationships, there has been the catalogue of disruption at an infra-church and inter-church level throughout history as well. The story of secessions and schisms – some of them justifiable, some not – is a significant element in the history of the church. What are we to make of such tragic tales of breakdown and fragmentation?

Nothing is to be gained from consigning them to the ever-growing pile under the great ecclesiastical carpet of church history where so much has been swept over the years. Whatever temporary relief may be gained from overlooking our failures and difficulties, ignoring them will not make them go away, or absolve the church from being responsible for them. It is far better to face them, on whatever scale, or with whatever embarrassment they may have occurred. The lessons learned from the *failures* of our forefathers can be as valuable as lessons learned from their greatest triumphs and successes. The biographies of the saints in the Bible do a much better job of portraying the lives of God's people than their successors in church history. They paint their subjects 'warts and all' and so cast us more than ever upon the free grace and mercy of God in Christ as the only basis of our boasting in earthly achievement. There is no room for hagiolatry in the Bible, only grace.

Thus, as we follow the contours of Christian fellowship in the Bible, we find again and again that it is torn apart by internal failure within the family of God. We also see, however, that God, wise and loving Father as he is, never lets his children off the hook when they disrupt the life of his family in this way. He makes them confront themselves and their failures. He shows them that the most insidious obstacles to a life of love and fellowship among the saints are actually found among the saints! It is the obstacles within the church which are the greatest hindrance to the fellowship of the church. Although the church is the community of the redeemed, so long as we think of it in terms of her life on earth we need always to qualify that statement slightly by saying, 'the community of redeemed sinners'. So long as the church is in the world, there will always be something of the world in the church.

As churches struggle with the issues of relationships within the Body of Christ, there are times when they can do no better than to stop and take a long, hard look at themselves in a mirror. As they look into God's Word (which describes itself as being mirror-like in its function, Jas. 1:22-25), they end up seeing themselves as God sees them and are put in a position to act accordingly.

When that happens it is inevitably a painful and embarrassing experience. Which of us likes seeing the ugly truth about ourselves in a purely physical sense as we take that first look at ourselves in the bathroom mirror each morning! How much more, then, when such self-appraisal is not just skin-deep but penetrates into the inner recesses of what we really are in ourselves. Despite the pain and shame involved, such exercises can only be profitable if they become instruments in God's hands to lead us on to better things individually and corporately. That is precisely what happens as Paul deals with the church in Corinth in the midst of their messy circumstances.

We have already made reference to the state of affairs in the Corinthian church which became the pretext for Paul's writing to them on at least three occasions, as well as going out of his way to visit them. After the initial greetings, pleasantries and prayers for their spiritual well-being, the apostle very quickly comes to his point in writing and brings into the open the fragmentation which had become the stuff of rumour and gossip in the wider Christian world. He spends much of his first epistle addressing the specific factors that had contributed to the divisions which were doing such damage in that church, but then he steps back and puts everything into perspective.

He addresses the problem itself using the imagery of the human body (1 Cor. 12:12-31). The illustration immediately captures the imagination because it conveys so succinctly the concept of the one and the many, but the apostle draws us even more dramatically into the thrust of what he is saying as he muses in almost grotesque fashion on a body which has gone wrong.

It is almost as though he is taking us into some museum of the freaks of nature as he muses on 'bodies' which are all eye, or all ear (12:17), or into a ward for the incapacitated as he talks of bodies with missing or unused parts. Yet the sheer distortion of bodies conceived in such a way drives home the point of what was going so horribly wrong in the church of the Isthmus. Paul's intention is not to pour scorn on the fellowship in Corinth, but to bring them to their senses. They had become so embroiled in the issues which were dividing the church that they had lost sight of the damage being done. Whatever principles had been at stake in the early stages of the dispute had long since been engulfed in the other issues which had arisen among them – the personal chemistry of the individuals and relationships of the situation being among the most obvious.

The verbal image Paul sets before them makes them look at themselves and the virtual ruin of the church of which they were a part. His purpose is ultimately remedial. Having seen what they were, these believers were being reminded, in a circuitous fashion, of what they ought to be. Not only were they being stirred again to act responsibly towards each other, but, more significantly, they were being thrust more earnestly upon the only One who gives the church its cohesion: the Christ whose body it is. Paul urges reflection on these matters on at least three levels.

Attitude to the Body as a Whole

Having confronted the plethora of issues which divide the congregation at Corinth, Paul brings their focus to bear upon that which unites them. In the midst of all their diversity there is an indisputable unity – one which takes account of their differences and explains many of them.

> For even as the body is one and *yet* has many members, and all the members of the body, though they are many, are one body, so also is Christ (1 Cor. 12:12).

In expressing this truth in that particular way (with the accent being on Christ, as opposed simply to the church), Paul is highlighting the divine purpose and provision in the midst of this facet of Christian experience. He wants his readers to see beyond the individual plane of salvation and set it in the context of the corporate experience of grace.

It is fundamentally wrong to try to isolate the individual from the whole. The diversity of the many who comprise the family of God is subsumed into the unity of the family in its completeness. The church possesses something *as* the body of Christ's people which it does not have merely as a collection of the individuals who happen to belong to it. What they are as they are spiritually knit together in Christ-dependant fellowship is on an altogether different realm from what they are privately and personally and in mere loose association with others in their experience of salvation. There is a spiritual dynamic involved which defines them uniquely as the people of God.

It is what the church is as a spiritual community – redeemed by a common Saviour, in union with him through a shared Spirit who is the very life of their soul, looking to a common Father – that sets it apart in the world and from the world. In the same way as a single beam of white light is split into the spectrum of colours as it passes through a prism; so, in reverse, the polychromatic body of the church traces its cohesion to the single ray of God's grace which shines through the cross into the present experience of the redeemed of all ages.

The 'bodies' which hold men and women together in a purely earthly sense can be ever so boring and monochrome in their appearance. A society of train-spotters, or a political party, or a guild of workers, can all look remarkably similar, whereas the sheer diversity of the church only serves to heighten awareness of the other-worldly bond that gives it its cohesion.

Such was true in a particular way in the city of Corinth, cultural melting pot that it was of the ancient world, where the church reflected the diversity of the community from which its converts had been saved. Paul was urging those very converts to recover that truth about themselves again and allow it once more to be the controlling influence in the way they related to one another and functioned as a church fellowship.

Sadly, it is just at this point that so many churches seem to lose their bearings. They allow the interests and concerns of individuals, or particular groups within the church, to override those of the church body as a whole. When the latter is subordinated to the former it is inevitable that something vital to the well-being of the church is going to be lost. In the redemptive purposes of God, the corporate is the ultimate.

Attitude to the Individual's Part in the Body

One cannot reflect upon the church as the body of Christ as an entity in itself without considering one's own place and function within that body. This was undoubtedly to the fore in Paul's thinking as he addressed the issues arising among God's people in Corinth. He wanted them to reappraise themselves individually in response to their reappraisal of the church collectively and corporately in relation to Christ. In so doing he expected them to mature in their self-understanding and their effectiveness in the faith as they conformed more closely to the pattern of church life Christ intended his people to follow.

It is quite possible that when a person embarks on such a course of reflection about their own place in the wider whole, they reach the conclusion that they do not actually belong to the body at all. If that is the case, although it may come as a shock, it is no bad thing. It is far better to realize that you are not in reality a member of the body of Christ than to live with the false sense of security that comes from the delusion that you are. If that happens, then it immediately brings a reappraisal of life with eternal implications. Those who presume themselves to be in, only to discover that they are out, must immediately avail themselves of the remedy God has provided through his Son – call on the name of the Lord and be saved! Take that step of faith which will lead to true incorporation into the life and fellowship of the church.

Assuming, however, that the answer to the question, 'Do I belong?' is, 'Yes', then how am I to work out my particular place and function in the body of Christ? It surely means appreciating ourselves as we are to begin with. Not that we should accept ourselves in our sinful state, but rather that we accept our unique individuality as being attributed to God. In the same way as the psalmist was able to say that he was 'fearfully and wonderfully made' (Ps. 139:14), so Paul urges his Corinthian friends to appreciate what they are as a specific part of the body – shaped and placed by God – and not keep wishing they were something else (1 Cor. 12:18).

Inevitably this will mean accepting the personal qualities we received when we came into the world. From the way we look, to the temperament we possess, our strengths to our weaknesses, we will recognize the hand of God in the way we are. Such self-image and self-worth can be grasped only in fellowship with Christ. In an age which places such a premium upon the advertising world's idea of the norm, the only way to really accept and appreciate ourselves is to see ourselves as part of God's bigger picture and purpose.

It will also mean appreciating what God has equipped us to be able to do. Sadly, years of inculcated self-deprecation in church life and an unhealthy mythology of the 'one-man ministry' have led to serious deficiencies in this realm. Christians have been conditioned to think more of what they cannot do than what they actually can. Such negativism is positively unbiblical. God not only wants us to see whether we are equipped to function as a hand, or a foot, or an eye – the gifts he has invested in us – but also the degree of giftedness we possess.

In the passage which deals with giftings in Romans, Paul draws attention to the fact that not all gifts are possessed in equal measure by God's children. There will be some Christians who possess the same gifts as other Christians, but to a different degree. We have them in accordance with the measure of grace God has seen fit to confer upon us (Rom. 12:6). Not all preachers will preach as well as others, those who practise hospitality will vary in the kind of welcome and attention they give to those they entertain. God does not expect us to be the best in any absolute sense, simply the best we can be within the limitations he has given us and the measure of giftedness we happen to possess. All too often people hold back from involvement and any attempt to use their abilities for fear of not being good enough. (There seems to have been something of that mentality present in Corinth.) The crucial thing is to be using what God has given within the context of the church.

There is something quite special about the way Paul puts the little bits, the weaker bits, the less honourable bits and the less presentable bits of the body into the limelight of God's purpose (1 Cor. 12:20-25). The very people and talents we are so inclined to write off as dispensable are in reality indispensable!

That kind of self-appreciation and mutual appreciation within the fellowship of the church serve to revolutionize the way in which the church functions and the impact it is likely to have in terms of its internal ministry to itself and external witness to the world.

When we look at ourselves and the body of Christ in this way we are drawn ultimately to God's incredible wisdom as the master builder of a world-wide, history-spanning church. Like some multi-million-piece jigsaw, God fashions, shapes and colours each individual piece so that it fits in where and how he wants it to and accomplishes what no other part ever could. Thus the contribution that each of his children will make to the life of his family will be unique and valuable beyond anything we might ever imagine when we think purely in individualistic and earthly categories. We will marvel at his workmanship.

By approaching our understanding of the nature of corporate life in the church in this way we can overcome the enormous obstacle of the wrong kind of humility and false assessment of the abilities of others that would impair the harmonious functioning of the body as a whole.

Attitude to Other Parts Around Us

The cohesion in this picture Paul is painting of the church is found in the way that all the parts of the body are amazingly knit together – joint to joint, sinew to sinew, tendon to tendon – to form a single complex whole. In endless permutations of relationships, the entire body is joined and held together with a unity that goes far beyond simply one part's being able to fit into the part that happens to be right next to it. The life of the body permeates the entire entity. So,

> ... if one member suffers, all the members suffer with it; if *one* member is honored, all the members rejoice with it (1 Cor. 12:26).

No single part of the body is disjoined from any other part of the body, each is caught up in the life and experience of the whole.

Clearly this must have an impact upon the life of the local congregation. It presents a challenge to those in leadership to ensure that all under their care are truly integrated into the life of the fellowship. Sadly, a model of church life which has reduced many churches to little more than preaching stations has mitigated against such integration. The cohesion that holds a church together in such cases is the magnetism of the present incumbent in the pulpit which, without minimizing the great blessing of pulpit ministry, can often overlook underlying issues in the life of a church which are to be addressed more through a pastoral dynamic than through the general ministry of the Word.

If we believe in the kind of responsible and courageous leadership which is modelled for us in Scripture and set before us in New Testament precept, then we can expect those who are charged with the task of shepherding the flock of Christ to take an active role in identifying needs and meeting them, recognizing gifts and putting them to use, and providing the kind of leadership which prevents those who are spiritually fit and healthy running ahead of the flock, or those who are spiritually weak lagging behind and losing their way.

It is not only the leadership, however, that will need to ruminate on the implications of this passage of Paul's. Those who are themselves members of the body of Christ, who have the requisite marks of God's grace in their life and experience, will see that the privilege of belonging to the church of Jesus Christ carries with it a whole range of responsibilities which cannot be ignored.

Fundamentally they will need to appreciate the responsibility of relationship into which they are placed. Church for them can never merely be a spiritual society to which they pay their dues and determine their own level of involvement. They belong by grace and they also function by grace in a set of relationships which owe their origin to grace.

It is particularly sad that many churches which have placed a high premium on orthodoxy of belief have placed

little store on the bond of fellowship in which that belief is
expressed and proclaimed. Far too many Christians are
'falling off the edge', as someone has observed, for want
of the kind of sympathy and support that one would expect
from the church that is described and defined by the New
Testament. Members of the body are hurting, but few of
their fellow members seem to feel their pain or want to
stand with them in their time of need. Whether it be through
marriages that are struggling to survive, children who have
become a handful to raise, or jobs that are becoming a
nightmare to sustain, Christians are being left to cope alone.

The principle does not stop there. The body that now
belongs to Christ through the redemptive price he paid on
the cross is not to be regarded atomistically as a series of
little unrelated congregations – it is one body, comprised
ultimately of one people of God saved throughout the entire
sweep of history from every people-group under heaven.
Even though that body has its local expression in a
multitude of sub-units which are the local church, they are
nevertheless part of an ultimate whole. Heaven will not be
segregated into the 'First Baptist', or 'Second Presbyterian'
churches of this world. It will simply be one vast company
of people 'which no man can number', that will enjoy
perfect unity and harmony in their worship of their Saviour-
Lamb and loving Father.

If that is the final goal to which we are being steered
above, then it follows that it must have some bearing upon
how we live together below. Some types of church have
institutionalized this principle as a spin-off of their
theology. Whether it be in Presbyterian or Episcopal
connections which centralize the authority and structures
of church life and care, or a more federal approach which

seeks to maintain a degree of local autonomy, there is a practical expression of connection between different local churches. Indeed, even where there is more emphasis placed on local autonomy than on wider relationships, there are really very few churches which so stress autonomy that they become effectively isolationist in their outlook. (Though sadly it does happen.)

Either way, no congregation which belongs to the true Church of Jesus Christ can dis-fellowship itself from the wider body into which its Redeemer has brought it through his blood. If that is to mean anything in practice – especially when it comes to reaching beyond particular denominational groupings – it requires churches to develop sensitivities to spiritual needs that will translate into appropriate contact and involvement, providing help to churches in need.

The Vexed Issue of Baptism

Many examples could be cited to illustrate how obstacles to fellowship and co-operation have arisen within and between churches. The landscape of the New Testament church is dominated by the obstacle between Jew and Gentile converts and churches that have one or other cultural ethos of those groupings. The equivalent blot on the ecclesiastical landscape for at least the past 300 years must surely be the debate over baptism.

Paul's comment to the Ephesians that there is 'one baptism' (Eph. 4:5) almost seems bizarre when we find churches and Christians who will stand almost four-square together on practically every area of biblical doctrine and yet (in some cases) refuse to share the Lord's Supper together because of radically differing interpretations of the sacrament of baptism. Something is wrong somewhere and the answer is not to smile piously and go on as though it didn't really matter.

Attempting to resolve the problem by setting out to convert the other side gets no results, as the harder one side tries to persuade, the more vigorous their counterparts become in defence! The route that opts for virtual separate existence is equally unsatisfactory because it leads to major constitutional and theological inconsistency when differing parties discover that they can have the sweetest of fellowship when they are on neutral turf! Such fellowship can be sustained only so long as no-one asks the awkward questions.

It would seem that a more meaningful way forward is to go down an avenue which is being explored quite courageously by a growing number of churches from both sides of the baptismal divide. This approach maintains the theological integrity of a particular church while giving biblical latitude for Christians who come along to it but do not share its views on the sacrament and the same kind of latitude for relationships with other churches which take a different view of the sacrament.

Surely it is possible to constitute belief and practice in the life of a church in such a way as to declare the church's position on baptism – safeguarding that position with a leadership committed to it by their own conviction – while allowing people to be members of the congregation in a way which acknowledges that a person's view on baptism does not determine their place in the Kingdom of God. Following on from that, surely the wider Reformed and Evangelical theology in which the respective doctrines of baptism are set is strong enough to maintain fellowship within the bounds of what is 'of first importance' (1 Cor. 15:3) while agreeing to differ on this particular of the faith. Baptismal integrity (of either hue) can be maintained at a congregational level without it becoming an obstacle to infra- and inter-church relationships.

In days when the massed ranks of unbelief are presenting a formidable threat to true Christianity in many parts of the world, it is time that those who love the truth in sincerity of heart came of age in their ability to handle their theology and look for more meaningful ways to stand together with those to whom we belong and stand against those who are the enemies of the cross.

Six paragraphs will never solve such a problem, but perhaps they can remind the church as it stands on the threshold of a new millennium that the new challenges which are facing us from without must make us think in fresh ways about old challenges from within. The body of Christ and the future of his work on earth is bigger than the issue of the theology of baptism.

Chapter Nine

'You Do not Struggle Against Flesh and Blood'
Opposition from Without

The controversies which have disrupted and divided the church have been complicated by personalizing the issues – often in a painful and distasteful way. In one sense it is right that the issues are personalized, but only insofar as the personality who is the true culprit in it all is the one on whom the focus is brought to bear. Paul brings in that focus in a most dramatic way in his closing remarks to the church in Ephesus – a church which, as we have seen already, was split up the middle over the contentious issue of Jewish and Gentile understandings of the faith. Whereas we might have expected the apostle to lean to one side or the other in the divide and suggest that it has the better of the argument, he points to neither group in itself, but rather the common enemy of them both.

> Finally, be strong in the Lord, and in the strength of His might. Put on the full armor of God, so that you will be able to stand firm against the schemes of the devil. For our struggle is not against flesh and blood, but against the rulers, against the powers, against the world forces of this darkness, against the spiritual *forces* of wickedness in the heavenly *places* (Eph. 6:10-12).

Behind every expression of the divisive and destructive power of evil, in the church or around it, is the ugly face of Satan.

He is the dark personality of the cosmic realm who is synonymous with chaos. It is his business to confuse and corrupt, divide and destroy, to undermine and usurp, leaving only a legacy of pain, degradation, sorrow and never-ending torment. Since his expulsion from the courts of heaven, he has been bent on opposing all that is good and all that is of God.

Paul wants his readers to walk with him, however briefly, onto the cosmic battlefield and appreciate for a moment the forces that are ranged against each other and see a few of the cameo-portraits of the foot-soldiers caught up in the teeth of battle.

The dramatic power of modern cinematography and the raised threshold of what cinema audiences are prepared to tolerate in terms of violence on the screen has allowed those who know nothing of the ugly reality of war to enter into the trenches and onto the beaches of the battlefields of history with an alarming sense of realism. Stephen Spielberg's 1998 epic, *Saving Private Ryan*, gave those who were not even born at the time of the Second World War an horrendous exposure to what it was like to come ashore in the Normandy landings in 1944: the vivid reality of it all is only intensified by the close character-studies which are woven through the film.

The crass poignancy of the violence of battle portrayed on screen is nothing compared to that experienced by those who have fought in the battles of history for real and then have returned to the scene of conflict years later and remembered comrades maimed and lost in the dreadful carnage.

The poignancy of this closing section of Paul's epistle to the Ephesians is powerful because he is not dealing with fictitious conflict, or conflict which has only been the experience of the few, but rather an all-too-real conflict which affects every living soul and which has eternal implications. Yet, incredibly, it is a conflict to which many, even among those who enjoy true spiritual enlightenment, are effectively blind. We fail to see beyond the immediacy of our struggles to the sinister powers which lie behind them all.

As we re-read Paul's manual for the Christian soldier – bearing in mind what he has already said about the conflicts within the fellowship of the church – there are a number of significant implications which emerge that have a bearing on the way Christians relate to one another in different settings.

Seeing Problems in Perspective

Difficulties within the church are often regarded and handled in such a way as to verge upon the ridiculous. Issues are taken out of context, blown out of proportion and turned into the means of all kinds of unnecessary damage for those caught up in them directly, not to mention the innocent bystanders who become the victims of any war, spiritual or otherwise. Paul wants us to see things in a way which will minimize the damage.

By taking us behind the scenes, as it were, in the problems that the church must face, Paul allows us a perspective on them which will inevitably affect the way we handle them. In the case of the church in Ephesus, the front issue of conflict of interest between two distinct traditions in the church is not to be the focus in itself, but rather the cause which lies behind it. Paul was demonstrating to both parties concerned that they were allowing themselves – to a large extent unwittingly – to play into the hands of a more sinister power. The surface issues of the tensions between cultures and traditions had become a mask for the underlying issue of an enemy who was opposed to both parties involved and the God they were serving.

Those who have been involved in the murky world of politics know only too well how those who have scaled the heights of political power and influence have done so, more often than not, at the expense of those who have become their pawns along the way. Naïve individuals have been taken in by power-brokers who will think nothing of using them for their own ends, only to discard them when their usefulness is over.

How much more so in the corridors of cosmic power, where its darkest ruler is well able to masquerade as 'an angel of light' (2 Cor. 11:14). Well Paul describes him as the one whose *modus operandi* is to scheme (Eph. 6:11). In the same way as he seduced Eve in her innocence with sweet words and enticing promises, only to abandon both her and her husband in the tragedy which was to follow (Gen. 3:1-7), so he continues to beguile those who are too quick to take things only at face value.

The implications of such a view on the realities we face as Christians, both in the world and in the church, are enormous. We will see the danger of being spiritually gullible and learn to look and think twice before we speak or act, appreciating that even the best of motives can fall prey to the worst of manipulation. More than anything else we might face, this view of our devilish opponent will drive home a deep appreciation of our need to be simultaneously shrewd and innocent (Matt. 10:16).

As he teases this thought out for his readers, Paul leaves them in no doubt as to the source of the opposition they face. Opposition emanates, not primarily from those who set themselves against us through their doctrine or their practice, but from the very pit of hell itself. To allow ourselves to be duped into merely humanizing the struggles of the church is to lose sight of the fact that we ourselves are part of the problem. Whether the conflict be over what we believe, or the way we live as Christians, none of us can pretend to be without fault on either score. That does not remove the responsibility to 'contend earnestly for the faith which was once for all handed down to the saints' (Jude 3), but rather tempers the way in which that contention is pursued. Jude himself goes on to highlight the humility and awe which should characterize true protagonists in this struggle by citing the dispute between Michael the archangel and the devil over the body of Moses (Jude 9). Those who dare to contend without insight and understanding of the wider issues involved do so at their own peril as well as that of their fellow believers.

The old maxim, 'Fools rush in where angels fear to tread', has been painfully true of many a church conflict. The worst spiritual folly is to fail to recognize, behind the opponents we meet along the way, the shadow of the one who is a roaring lion, who 'prowls about ... seeking someone to devour' (1 Pet. 5:8), or to fail to remember that this same shadowy figure is the father of lies whose native language is that of deceit and whose ultimate purpose from the beginning has been murder (John 8:44).

In the long-running 'troubles' of Ulster, in which the

focus of world and media attention has so often been on terrorist atrocities, an officer involved in the intelligence service once said, 'When the truth finally comes out, people will be amazed at who the real godfathers of terrorism are!' There is more to the struggle than meets the eye. So with all conflict in the spiritual realm, it too is complex and the godfather of evil will always do his utmost to conceal his own identity as the one who spawns division and its consequences.

Paul not only wants us to be aware of the ultimate source of opposition in this conflict, but also its true nature: 'Our struggle is not against flesh and blood' (Eph. 6:12). If that were the case, then our flesh and blood resources would be sufficient in themselves to resolve the struggles that we face. It is often a source of great perplexity that differences, which seem so obviously resolvable to simple logic, either between Christians within a church, or between denominations, have a nasty habit of never going away. Churches which hold to the same confessional standards, hold to the same practices in worship and share the same passion for the same gospel in the same locality can continue a virtually separate existence in a way which defies comprehension.

The explanation for this bizarre phenomenon lies precisely in the fact that these are not problems of mere logic or simple desire or determination. It is the reality of a spiritually hostile power which can readily take advantage of the enemy within – the lingering propensity to sin which resides in every Christian. The nature of the opponent ranged against us in the faith must determine the nature of the help to which we must turn if we are to overcome in the midst of evil, namely the mighty power of God himself (Eph. 6:10).

Paul uses similar language in his comments to the embattled congregation in Corinth, reminding them that 'the weapons of our warfare are not of the flesh, but divinely powerful for the destruction of fortresses' (2 Cor. 10:4). The divisions within their fellowship – every bit as much as their failures in the faith – could be remedied only by a means that was equal to the threat: the resources which God supplies. We will come on to consider that more closely a bit further on, but there is one more aspect of the opposition to which Paul draws our attention.

He wants to leave us in no doubt as to the scale of the opposition. In the same way as we might gaze up into the starry sky at night, we are to look up into the unseen realities of 'the heavenlies' (Eph. 6:12, lit.), and see a formidable array of threatening powers that are clearly visible only in the light of God's Word. It is as though there is a fearsome battle-formation of all kinds of configurations of evil which act in concert to pursue the evil schemes of their satanic general. Paul does not want the church to underestimate for a moment the scale of hostilities it is facing. Like the ominous shadow cast across the landscape by an advancing weather front, so is the shadow cast across the church by the combined forces of evil.

When the church is complacent towards these realities, she is at her weakest and will allow herself to be overtaken by all that will divide her ranks and disrupt her best efforts. But when she is alert – even in her weakest condition – God's people will stand together in dependence upon God in a way which will make her invincible in the face of the rising tide of evil.

Appreciating the Difference Between Enemies and Allies
With the advance of modern techniques in warfare which
pride themselves in pin-point accuracy, the tragedy of death
and injury as the result of 'friendly fire' have come to the
fore more than ever before. Quite apart from the dreadful
misnomer of such a phenomenon, it serves as a chilling
and graphic illustration of what continues to happen in the
church despite centuries of refinement in theological
understanding and the experience of the Christian life. The
church seems to be able to do far more damage to herself
and her witness through so-called 'friendly fire' than
through the direct assaults that Satan would mount against
her. Those who serve in the ranks of the army of the Lord
need to be skilled in discerning the difference between ally
and enemy.

It is interesting that Jesus' response to his disciples'
questions about perceived opponents sounds almost
simplistic: '... he who is not against you is for you' (Luke
9:50). Just because someone else who was driving out evil
spirits did not 'follow along with' the disciples, they tried
to stop him, fearing rivalry or opportunism or worse. Such
paranoia is commonplace in many Christian circles. The
criteria for judging faithfulness in others becomes, not the
objective standard of the gospel, but the subjective standard
of 'how *we* do things'. We manage to canonize our own
traditions and ways and in so doing alienate many who are
truly brothers in Christ.

As the ease of contact between nations and cultures
brings Christians from diverse backgrounds into more
frequent contact with each other, the most immediate
impression will often be of the differences which exist
between those from varied backgrounds. The cultural

clothing and baggage which inevitably surround spiritual life as much as any other aspect of life will draw attention before there is time to compare what is believed and cherished by each party. Just because there may not be precise correspondence between the way things appear on the surface, it does not mean that there is significant difference in reality.

Although Jesus could easily have introduced all kinds of qualifications and caveats to warn against those who make a spurious claim to discipleship (as he does elsewhere),[9] he shows that his way is to begin by giving those who act in his name the benefit of the doubt. We ought to manifest that true spirit of Christian love, by believing the best and hoping for the best (1 Cor. 13:7).

The church is in great need of deliverance from the spirit of suspicion and cynicism that all too often characterizes its life. Such negativism mitigates against the building of bridges within the Christian community and restoring those who do need to be shown 'the way of God more accurately' (Acts 18:26) and often leads to a hardening of heart and attitude which bears little resemblance to Christ. In the midst of the many casualties of church conflicts and disagreements there have been many who have not differed in a substantial way with brothers and sisters in terms of belief, but who have ended up being alienated because of the way in which they have been treated. As has been said already, the gospel puts a constraint not just on *what* we believe, but the *way* in which we hold and defend our beliefs.

The apostle Paul adopts a similarly straightforward approach in the volatile situation in Corinth. Despite the various factions which had emerged within the fellowship there, he reduces the crucial test for true membership of

the body of Christ to: 'no one can say, "Jesus is Lord,"
except by the Holy Spirit' (1 Cor. 12:3). The difficulties
which had caused that church to become dysfunctional had
been exacerbated by an unhealthy spirit which was calling
into question the reality of spiritual experience in an unfair
manner.

None of this takes away the fact that there will always
be people and churches which claim to be Christian, but
which in reality are not. There was a Judas among the
Twelve; there were those of whom a pastor said, 'They
went out from us, but they were not *really* of us' (1 John
2:19); there have been entire congregations like that of
Sardis which have a reputation of spiritual life but in reality
are dead (Rev. 3:1). There will always be the need to guard
against false prophets and teachers, to be alert to the spirit
of antichrist and ultimately 'test the spirits to see whether
they are from God' (1 John 4:1). But, at the same time,
such vigilance will not be so crude as to leave the weak
and wounded of the family of God standing out in the cold.
Even with the internal complexities in the church which
were faced in John's day, the test of spiritual authenticity
did not become more complicated. It was still, 'By this
you know the Spirit of God: every spirit that confesses
that Jesus Christ has come in the flesh is from God' (1
John 4:2). We need to be able to distinguish true friend
from foe in this spiritual battle.

Using the Resources Placed at our Disposal

As we return to Paul's injunction to the Ephesian church as
he imparts God's battle-orders to God's people, we cannot
help but be struck by the simplicity of the spiritual 'kit'
which is supplied to the spiritual warrior. In an age of

spiritual sophistication in the evangelical world, many of the simplest elements of spiritual equipment provided for the battle have been foolishly discarded at great personal cost.

The strength for the fight is not found in any human source, but in God and in fellowship with him through his Son (Eph. 6:10). There is no substitute for a close walk with Jesus.

Too many churches have fallen prey to the ideas and methods of an image-conscious age. Church-growth theology has often placed such an emphasis on ethos and presentation that the most basic element of faith in God has been eclipsed, personal and public prayer has been neglected and the work of God has suffered. The frightening thing about such a scenario is that the spiritual spin-doctors who stage-manage such an approach to church work are unable to recognize when their 'results' are not real. Even when failure stares them in the face, they manage to put the most positive gloss on it and persevere regardless.

In many situations the idea of needing to spend time each day as Christians in a quiet place with God in prayer and for Bible-reading has come to be regarded as a quaint relic from a previous age of Christian experience. The notion that we might benefit in not only beginning, but also ending God's day in God's house, around God's Word, with God's people is rapidly becoming outmoded. Yet the corresponding decline in spiritual vitality, missionary zeal and meaningful impact on a secular world seems to go virtually unnoticed.

Only time will tell how far the church must go under her own steam before she realizes that her own innate resources are no match for the task that God has given and the battle into which she has been plunged. Sadly there will be too much spiritual wreckage along the way before God's people are brought to their senses and are brought back to him in humble, prayerful dependence.

In a sophisticated military age of cruise missiles, laser-guided bombs and stand-off combat, the foot soldier still needs and values his rifle, kit-bag and helmet. God's army is no different. The basic essentials are indispensable: truth, righteousness and peace (all of which are the constituents of the gospel), faith, salvation and the Bible, bound together with the most tangible expression of our dependence on God through prayer (Eph. 6:13-18). They are needed, not in part, but as a whole. They are provided, not for parade dress, but warfare in the spiritual trenches.

The blame for too many of our defeats and much of our ineffectiveness as Christians lies at our own feet. We simply have not made use of what God has supplied, and the enemy has had a field day.

In terms of what this means for the unity of God's people, it is striking to note that all the elements of the Christian soldier's equipment have a unifying impact on his or her relationship with others. The truth has its own magnetic influence on all who love the truth. The righteousness and peace which are found in Christ turn all who love him away from themselves to him and to others who have found their peace in him. Those who are learning to live by faith will have a kindred spirit with others who share the same struggle. Those who have truly experienced salvation by God's grace will soon recognize others whose testimony is the same. Those for whom the Spirit's greatest gift is his Bible-Sword will, by Spirit-imparted instinct, gravitate towards others who have come to cherish this remarkable weapon.

Most of all, those who really belong to God will pray together. Prayer – even as a personal exercise – is never an individual pursuit. As Jesus teaches us to pray, '*Our* Father who art in heaven ...' (Matt. 6:9), he instils into his children the persistent need to pray with and for their brothers and sisters in God's family. Thus, quite simply, praying together can be the most effective medicine for healing the damaging wounds inflicted upon the fellowship of the church.

God has provided a battle-kit which is more than adequate for the needs of his troops on the ground. It is for us to make full use of that provision that we might stand together against a common enemy and not against each other to the enemy's delight.

Chapter Ten

God's New Community
The Church of the Different Dimension

There is a dimension in the life of the universal church which can be overlooked very easily and yet which has a significant bearing on how we are to understand our place and our responsibility within that body. It is that point at which the community of God's people on earth touches that of his people who are in heaven. Although in one sense they belong to two very different spheres, in reality they belong to one and the same: a dimension of being which straddles both worlds.

Although such an insight into the life of the church might seem esoteric and completely removed from the daily grind of the experience of Christian living, it is a truth which features prominently in the writings of the apostle Paul and it is also a truth which is brought to bear in a most practical way on the struggle of the Christian life in the book of Hebrews. Paul writes that since we are joined to Christ by faith and through his Spirit, we are therefore seated with him in the heavenly places and are the recipients of all spiritual blessings in that context by virtue of our relationship with him (Eph. 1:3; 2:6). The writer to the Hebrews asserts that the church of God on earth assembles, not in disparate, isolated congregations, but *together* it comes to,

> Mount Zion and to the city of the living God, the heavenly
> Jerusalem, and to myriads of angels, to the general assembly and
> church of the first-born who are enrolled in heaven, and to
> God, the Judge of all, and to the spirits of the righteous made
> perfect, and to Jesus, the mediator of a new covenant, and to the
> sprinkled blood, which speaks better than the blood of Abel
> (Heb. 12:22-24).

The weight of significance that this claim was to have upon the situation faced by the congregations addressed in this epistle was and continues to be far-reaching.

There is an obvious importance which attaches to this great assertion because it gives us a glimpse into the mysterious strand of reality that bridges the divide between existence in space and time, on the one hand, and existence in the world to come, on the other. As God provides insight through his revelation of this realm, we see that it is more than simply a chronological or sequential divide – a point which is passed at the moment of physical death – but is one in which these two realms of being converge and relate. Such insights are beyond the scope of conventional scientific investigation and belong to that order of things which are only accessible because of God's revelation. Although he has not given this aspect of his truth the same prominence as he has with other aspects (because it is clearly the kind of teaching that could easily become the stuff of esoteric speculation), he has brought it to our attention as an important element in his redemptive purpose, therefore it should not be ignored.

The immediate significance of this truth is to be found in the context in which it is given in the letter to the Hebrews. We need to bear in mind that this epistle was addressed to believers who were hard pressed in the faith.

They had been exposed, not only to opposition from without (through persecution which had entailed the confiscation of property, imprisonment and even torture and death), but also to opposition from within. The ravages of false teachers and false prophets were taking their toll and the church was falling prey to confusion and perplexity to such an extent that many of the original addressees of this letter were on the point of reverting to their roots in Judaism.

The sheer force of circumstances for these believers was tending towards dividing and atomizing the church. Clearly there were some who had already fallen by the wayside as far as regular attendance at public worship was concerned (Heb. 10:25) and the general nature of the epistle made it clear that the problems of one at that time were the problem of all. Thus the need to recover a meaningful cohesion among the Christian community was paramount in order to encourage those who belonged to it. For that reason, the author takes them beyond the level of the visible unity (or lack of it) of the church in the world, to the glorious unity of which they were a part in God's wider scheme of things.

The church of our day needs to be reminded just as much of what God is doing at this present time in his work among his people, as of what he will ultimately accomplish when his work is finally complete and his people in the age of eternity finally become 'the Church Triumphant'.

The Church of the New Dimension
The author of Hebrews is at pains to enable his readers to appreciate the fact that they belong to something which is of an altogether different order from anything occurring naturally in the world, or, for that matter, from anything

that was the norm for the experience of the people of God prior to Christ's coming into the world. There is something unique and distinctive about the church as the people of God which is inextricably linked to Christ's coming into the world and that event's consequence: the outpouring of his Holy Spirit. The desire of these Hebrew Christians, to revert to a Judaism which was akin to the kind of faith found in Old Testament times, meant it was vital to show them that not even the faith of Moses and the patriarchs would have been complete if it were not in some way connected to the fulfilment of God's promise in the coming of God's Son.

The overall thrust of this concern is to demonstrate that the community of the faithful is nothing less than the church of the new dimension – a dimension in which all things are held together in Christ in the truest and fullest possible sense (Col. 1:17).

This insight into the collective identity of the people of God has been hinted at in an earlier chapter in Hebrews when it speaks of those who have,

> ... been enlightened and have tasted of the heavenly gift and have been made partakers of the Holy Spirit, and have tasted the good word of God and the powers of the age to come (Heb. 6:4-5).

Although the direct reference in that context is to those who have been incredibly close to true conversion, but have subsequently fallen away, the language is consistent with what is entailed in an experience of God's grace that genuinely does lead to salvation and a place in his Kingdom. The use of the expression, 'have tasted of the powers of the age to come', certainly contains a strong echo of Paul's designation of believers in the New

Testament epoch as being those 'upon whom the ends of the ages have come' (1 Cor. 10:11). Taken together it is clear that these expressions point to true Christian experience as being brought by God's grace into a new realm of existence and life by means of all he has accomplished through the redemptive work of his Son and the regenerating influence of his Spirit.

All of this then tallies with the whole range of references throughout the New Testament which indicate (a) that the Kingdom of heaven and of God is antithetical to that of this present fallen world, (b) that the present evil age in which we live is completely at odds with the new age and order of things to which we belong in Christ, and (c) that though the believer is in the world, he or she is no longer of it, their citizenship is in heaven. The people of God hold title to what this world can never know by nature, apart from God's saving grace and intervention.

In the context of the unfolding argument in Hebrews, the enfeebled believers who were reading these words were encouraged by the great sense of solidarity they felt with the great Old Testament saints they so much admired. Having alluded directly to the Old Testament hall of fame of the faithful (in which 'faithful' is as much the rightful designate of the humblest believer as the most prominent servant of God), the writer argues that these 'heroes' of the faith could not have been made perfect in isolation from the New Testament believers to whom he was writing (Heb. 11:40). The force of the argument is quite overwhelming in that it demonstrates the utter oneness of the people of God – a oneness which spans both Testaments and the redemptive epochs they represent – and also the absolute uniqueness of God's way of redemption, since all of this finds its focus in Jesus Christ.

He wants these Hebrew Christians to grasp the fact that far from them needing to revert to something which belonged to a former age of God's unfolding salvation, those who were part of that former age had been longing for the days of fulfilment which only arrived with the incarnation of Christ. It was vital, therefore, for these Christians to rise above the parochial confines of the limitations they were placing on their understanding of the church and appreciate that they belonged to something of great and glorious proportions, bound up with the dramatic saving grace of God.

That amazing truth continues to challenge believers of every age to realize that they belong to a body which is infinitely bigger and better than anything manifest merely on the earth. The church in this world is inseparably bound to the church of the world to come and together in the Lord Jesus Christ we represent the reality of a new dimension in the present world and universe: that of God's new creation.

This incredible insight into the dimensions of God's saving purpose speaks volumes to a generation which has become hopelessly confused over the meaning of life and which struggles with the stark reality of human mortality. It is not just in the world at large, which is increasingly entranced and intoxicated by New Age mysticism masquerading in the guise of 'spirituality', but also in the church itself among people who ought to know better, that the horizons of life in this world have loomed so large as to virtually eclipse the overriding horizons of their ultimate destiny in the age to come.

God wants us to see things as they really are in order that his people might live together before a watching world in the way he really wants them to. We would do well to develop this, first of all in the context of Hebrews and then in the wider application to the life of the church in general.

The Encouragement of What is Yet to Be

The glorious mystery of the Kingdom of God and his great salvation is that the wonder of the 'there and then' has broken through into our experience of the 'here and now'. Two worlds which are essentially distinct have become conjoined in God's redemptive intervention in a world which is under his curse and hurtling towards judgement.

The saving grace of justification is nothing less than the righteous declaration of acquittal on the Day of Judgement being announced and enjoyed before the event. The standing of believers as 'saints' – the holy ones of God – amounts quite simply to their being set apart from the world for the Lord. Their distinctive position is made manifest in that the moral and spiritual characteristics of life in that other world become the traits of life of those who have yet to go there. The Kingdom of God is the presence of the saving, sovereign rule of God in the midst of the fallen and rebellious world of men.

There has been an invasion of grace. There has been an intrusion of what is yet to be into the world of what is presently experienced. To belong to the church is to be part of what has been aptly described as 'a colony of heaven'. Hence, when those who belong to that colony assemble on earth for worship and fellowship, they cannot do so without experiencing a communion with God and with his people which stretches beyond the borders of what is earthly to what is in its very essence heavenly.

In the same way as those who are young in the faith

need the company, example and instruction of those who
are more mature in order to encourage them along the way
of progress in the Christian life, so all believers in this
world need the encouragement of their brothers and sisters
who have already reached their heavenly home to spur them
on to the very end. This is true, not in the sense, as some
believe, of super-saints acting as intercessory mediators
for Christians on earth, but rather in the fact of their glorified
state and the reality of our oneness with them providing a
profound encouragement that the God who begins a good
work in a life will not fail to bring it to its glorious
completion (Phil. 1:6).

It stands to reason that being able to grasp these unseen
realities involves faith, but then that is the very heart of the
Christian life. It is, as the author of Hebrews has already
said in his preface to the catalogue of the faithful, 'the
assurance of things hoped for, the conviction of things not
seen' (Heb. 11:1). He is not advocating the kind of faith
which is tantamount to intellectual suicide and leaping into
the dark, but rather that which takes God's self-revelation
at face value and trusts both him and it.

It is that kind of faith which desperately needs to be
restored to the life of the church in an age which is fixated
with the tangible. Conversion and the process of growing
up in the Christian life have all too often become focused
on factors which are visible and subject to manipulation as
opposed to the great unseen realities to which we are
pointed in the gospel. When faith is concentrated in the
material realm, it is bound to leave itself wide open to the
ever fluctuating influence of such an unstable realm. As
the writer of Hebrews wants his readers to appreciate, faith
needs a firm anchorage that will keep us through the

vicissitudes of life in this world (Heb. 6:19). This means going 'within the veil' to God and to all that is secured by him through his Son in heaven.

It is only in that realm and in God and his unfailing purposes in salvation that we can find genuine encouragement in the Christian life. There we find the goal for which we are aiming, a goal which entails the perfect unity of those whom God has redeemed.

The Challenge of What We Need to Be

The reminder of these things not only serves to encourage us with the knowledge that what God begins, he always completes, but also provides us with a challenge. If we are allowed even the smallest of glimpses of what the church will become when its members pass into that glorified state on the other side of death, then we are denied the right to countenance anything in the church below that would be in conflict with the life of the church above. Indeed, if our fellowship is truly with those who are the glorified saints on earth – those who enjoy perfect unity and harmony with God and with each other – then it should be a constant source of sorrow to those who remain on earth that we fall short of what God intends.

In the context of internal strife among Christians and churches this has a very direct and pertinent bearing. Even by the standards of simple logic, if we are to share heaven with those who are brothers and sisters in Christ and do so in love and harmony, then we must aim to cultivate such fellowship and harmony on earth.

There is simply no room for the assertion that 'I *cannot* love ...', or, 'I *cannot* forgive ...', when what we really mean is, 'I *will* not ...' The vast majority of divisions between Christians and between churches are issues of sanctification first and foremost. Far from being insoluble issues (the Bible does not know of such things, given the resources of grace), they are simply issues which require our determined and persistent labours to resolve.

The beauty of the gospel is that *all* we need for life and godliness – collectively as much as individually – is made available through Jesus Christ (2 Pet. 1:3). The fullness of God's provision for our need carries with it the commensurate weight of responsibility to make full use of the resources placed at our disposal in Christ by his word and by his Spirit. Therefore, as we contemplate our fellowship with the unseen host of those who have passed on before us to glory and as we share with them in the worship of the heavenly realm, we face the challenge of pursuing the 'peace with all men, and ... sanctification' at every level of Christian experience which is essential for those who would see God (Heb. 12:14).

The Assurance of How We are Enabled to Be

The main thrust of what the author of Hebrews is saying is that the faith of those who remained true to the end and are now in the immediate presence of their Saviour was firmly fixed in him and in his faithfulness to his covenant promises. The fact that God did not renege on his word to these believing people provides hope and certainty that he will likewise remain true to those who have yet to enter that perfected state of Christian experience.

The danger for all who profess faith is that they place their confidence, not in Christ, but in themselves, or in the fact that they have believed. Indeed, it is alarming to see the way in which so many pastoral attempts to deal with the problems of doubt and lack of assurance in the Christian life do not actually point people to the Saviour, but to themselves and in so doing only deepen their problems!

Hebrews leaves us in no doubt that the One who has made the promise 'is faithful' (Heb. 10:23). Thus, even someone of weak faith like Sarah, facing in human terms the impossible, was nevertheless blessed amazingly because, 'she considered Him faithful who had promised' (Heb. 11:11). The enabling to achieve through faith is all from God.

As we have suggested already, so many of the obstacles to resolving disputes and difficulties among believers arise from the fact that they seem at face value to be insurmountable. Especially in situations where genuine efforts to bring about reconciliation have come to nothing, the temptation is simply to give up trying. When we are reminded that the ability to find resolution has been supplied to us as part of God's gift of salvation, then we realize that we can never give up.

It is one of the loveliest little details of the New Testament record to see that even deep and long-standing rifts between Christians can be sorted out with time and through grace. The dispute between Paul and Barnabas over John Mark which sundered such an effective missionary team (Acts 15:39), could easily have been carried by the apostle to the grave. Yet, as Paul plans for the ongoing work of the gospel, despite the likelihood of his imminent death, he specifically asks that Mark be brought to him because he was useful for service (2 Tim. 4:11). We are not told precisely how the rift was healed, but we do know that that relationship was restored beyond what it had been prior to the disagreement.

Christians are enabled to persevere with God and with

each other in the face of all such obstacles and difficulties in the Christian life simply because God has promised to persevere with them. As we look ahead to those who have gone before us into glory and fix our eyes upon the One who has saved them, kept them and brought them there, then we too will find the help to press on to that which God has promised.

It is vital that we hold on to the fact that the church on earth is inseparably united to the glorified church in heaven if we are to keep our nerve and hold to our God-given bearings as we work out our salvation in the present evil age. The discouragements which might so easily overwhelm us are themselves overwhelmed by the reminder of brothers and sisters who have made it home and have received God's consummate blessing. We fix our eyes, not on what is seen and what can only discourage, but on what is unseen, yet which alone can guarantee our future.

The Power to Forgive
Returning finally to the passage in Hebrews, it is of critical significance that the text tells us that we come ultimately 'to the sprinkled blood, which speaks better than the blood of Abel' (Heb. 12:24). The place of any person in the hallowed company of those who worship in God's presence is entirely dependent upon the blood of Jesus Christ who is the mediator of the new and better covenant.

Whereas the blood of Abel cries out for vengeance, the blood of Jesus calls for pardon. As he has reconciled his believing people to God through the sacrifice of Calvary, providing God with the just basis to forgive and accept them as righteous on account of Christ and his perfect righteousness, so also he provides the reason for mutual forgiveness within the fellowship of the saints.

As this assembly of the saints are joined in fellowship with God through his pardoning grace, despite the fact that their sins and offences are divisive by nature, they are held together with each other, by their God-given power and duty to forgive others, even as God has forgiven them.

It is the power of forgiveness and the power to forgive which are such significant elements in the life of the body of Christ. Quite simply, there can be no harmony within the body without it. Therefore, we have every reason to fix our eyes upon Jesus as the author and finisher of our faith. He alone, through his sacrifice, has demolished all that sunders fellowship with God and with our fellow human beings.

Chapter Eleven

'Spare No Effort'
Commitment to Hard Labour

The charge could well be levelled against much that has been said so far that it appears to cast caution to the wind and invite the very recklessness in belief that has fuelled so much of the fragmentation in evangelical Christianity in the twentieth century. Surely one of the distinguishing features of genuine evangelical faith is its ability to discern and give no quarter to anyone or anything that would jeopardize the gospel? If such an accusation is envisaged, then it must also be levelled at what God himself has said in his own Word.

In the last analysis, it is Scripture alone that sets the agenda for Christians and the church in terms of what they must believe and how they should live. At many points that leaves God's people living with a tension that is not always neatly or easily resolved. To face that tension in the way that the Pharisees chose to face it, by fencing God's law with their own law and separating so far from others who professed to know and love God (no matter how noble their motives may have been), is to chart a course for spiritual fossilization. It has been astutely observed that the Pharisees were the evangelical party of their day: obsessed with theological orthodoxy, moral rectitude and ecclesiastical purity. Yet their zeal to pursue these ends led them to step beyond the boundaries set by the very Word they claimed to cherish so dearly. In the end, whatever spiritual vitality there may have been in the founding fathers of the movement, it was finally sapped and replaced by something that was but 'rules taught by men' (Matt. 15:9).[10] So many churches and denominations which began with the finest evangelical credentials have simply degenerated over the years into lifeless monuments to their former glory. In so doing, more often than not, they have lost the spirit of catholicity which marked their spiritual roots; a catholicity which rejoiced in the gospel more than in ecclesiastical distinctives as the key to their identity.

Thus, as we receive what God gives us in his Word, we receive also the weight he attaches to the various elements of his message. We will not be surprised that the centre of gravity of God's Word is to be found in God's own Son who is the Word of God incarnate. But we may be surprised to find just how close to the centre of gravity God places the responsibility he himself lays upon his people to live in peace and harmony with one another for the glory of his Son and the furtherance of his kingdom on earth.

Thus, to return to the epistle in which we began – the epistle to the church in Ephesus and its surrounding regions – we simply cannot play down the importance attached to the apostolic injunction to pursue the unity of the Spirit in the bond of peace (Eph. 4:3). When we couple together the location of this injunction (at the start of that portion of the letter which is devoted to application of the truth already expounded) with the strength of language that Paul employs ('spare no effort'), we begin to appreciate that this is no incidental detail which the church can gloss over. No matter how uncomfortable or embarrassed it may make us feel, we are confronted with something that God deems to be of vital importance.

The choice of words puts the accent on the *effort* that this whole exercise will inevitably involve. This is not something which comes either naturally or easily. There is an obvious, albeit tacit, implication that there are bound to be frustrations and disappointments along the way, but these must not deter God's people from pursuing God's calling at this most critical point in the outworking of God's great salvation in their corporate life on earth.

More than ever there is a need to re-emphasize these truths to the church because of what was described as 'the small-business mentality' by Donald MacLeod in his days as the editor of *The Monthly Record* of the Free Church of Scotland. In the same way as small businesses have often had a blinkered outlook on their place in the world of commerce, to their own ultimate cost and effectiveness, so also churches and denominations can become so self-absorbed that they lose sight of the very reason they were called into existence in the fallen world of men. No church was ever meant to be a 'small business' in pursuit of its own little ends. Every local and individual expression of the church is by definition part of something greater and it cannot afford to lose sight of its wider affiliation and responsibilities.

Evangelical Christianity – especially of the more conservative and theologically minded variety – has all too often gone down this very road with painful consequences for its own experience and with embarrassing consequences for the witness it presents to the world. It has allowed itself to become calloused and crusty in the way it has held the very gospel truths which are its hall-mark. The end-product is not a life which will 'adorn the doctrine of God our Saviour' (Tit. 2:10), but, rather, one which will bring it into disrepute. In its handling of a gospel which hinges upon grace, that grace has often been noticeable by its absence in the life and relationships of the church. For a gospel which celebrates forgiveness from God, such corresponding forgiveness has all too often been reluctantly imparted in our dealings with our fellow believers and fellow men. The dynamic of God's message of salvation, as we have already noted, is by its very nature something which needs to be seen as well as heard in order to be believed. The church needs to reflect again on this aspect of her calling and commit herself to walking worthy of it.

As we try to draw together some of the strands of what has been covered in the preceding pages, it might be helpful to offer a few practical reflections and even share some wistful dreams.

Beginning With What is Possible

No matter where we happen to be on the spectrum of relationships covered in this book, if we are to move beyond that point, we need to start where we are already. We are dealing with issues which by their very nature involve other people, and this means that we cannot attempt to relate in the realm of our dreams, only in the harsh realities of present experience.

For some that starting point will be in the context of rich and meaningful fellowship within congregations and between churches at various levels. The challenge for them will be to cherish and guard what they have and share something of their vision with others in God's family around them. Such joys and blessings of life in the church are all too easily taken for granted and all too quickly stolen by unexpected means. Hence Paul's injunction to the Ephesians is to '*preserve* the unity of the Spirit ...' (Eph. 4:3). It is one of the spiritual blessings of the heavenly realms which is a foretaste of the harmony and peace of heaven itself and the devil will do his utmost to disrupt and destroy our experience of it here on earth.

For other people, their starting point will be completely different. Perhaps on account of painful experiences of division and even schism in church life or in a wider fellowship of churches, there are wounds that are deep and suspicions that are understandably strong. Perhaps because of a prevailing theological and ecclesiastical tradition there is a natural tendency towards isolationism. Whatever the precise cause, broadening and deepening the bonds of Christian fellowship does not come easily to a lot of Christian people and they would rather shy away from it than take the risks involved in reaching out.

In these more difficult situations it would be naïve to the point of madness to presume that new and better relationships will begin to happen without at least some measure of pain and perplexity. Hence being aware of the sensitivities involved will, in its own simple, yet necessary way, temper all efforts to pursue them. Nevertheless, none of these things should impede those first steps which would lead into a deeper appreciation of the breadth of God's true family. Some obvious guidelines are worth noting in order to find a footing.

Start with those who are closest! In the setting of a local congregation where there has been strife and division, there are always some people to whom we find it difficult to relate. That should not necessarily make us feel guilty. There is a personal chemistry involved in all relationships which enables us to relate more easily to one person than to another. That being the case, it is always more sensible to start strengthening bonds of fellowship initially with those with whom we can have some rapport. It becomes wrong, however, when we refuse to go beyond that self-determined circle to explore the true expanse of the family in which God has placed us.

That same principle applies in a slightly different way when it comes to developing links between churches. For churches that have not been used to wider associations or that have been defined by deeply held convictions about baptism, or a particular statement of faith, it would hardly be a promising move to attempt, by way of a first step, to reach out to other churches that do not share their convictions. Again it is wiser to start with the possible. Other churches with similar concerns and a similar ethos are the obvious candidates for initial broader contact. Having crossed that hurdle, however, the next challenge is to reach as far in fellowship as the limits of the gospel will allow.

Evangelicalism around the world has been blessed over the last 150 years and longer with a growing number of associations and groups which exist to foster inter-church relations within a recognized and defined framework of belief and practice. Such groupings provide excellent opportunities to enter and enjoy a fuller experience of church fellowship and co-operation for churches which might otherwise be left out on a limb.

Surely the dream we all should cherish, however, is that the Reformed and Evangelical doctrine of the church should so come of age that it might move beyond the theoretical unity that it is bound to confess from Scripture and translate into a genuine union of churches. A union which allows for the measure of local autonomy that Scripture allows for churches while not allowing that to detract from the overall corporate identity of the church which is recognizable even to a fallen world. Such a dream would inevitably mean a willingness to insist only on those primary truths which are of the essence of the gospel, while allowing liberty of conscience on secondary issues. It would also mean facing the significant, but far from insurmountable, challenge of providing an ecclesiastical framework which did not have a particular theology of baptism as its defining element.

The spiritual climate of the world in which we live is changing rapidly. The focus of Christianity is on the move again away from the western world, so influenced by the Reformation, to so-called Third-World countries in which the church is experiencing rapid expansion. In face of these changes, the need for true unity is almost being forced upon us. One can envisage the day when true Christian fellowship will be so hard to find in some areas and opposition to the church so strong, that those who love the gospel will no longer be able to afford the luxury of pursuing their own particular ends, but instead will gladly welcome the fellowship of any true brother in Christ.

Sustaining the Vision
In the same way as the greatest threat to family relationships comes when family members take those relationships for granted and simply neglect the responsibilities which are attached to them, so with the family of God. When, as

members of that wider family circle, we allow ourselves
to become distracted and preoccupied with our own
particular concerns and interests, strife is often not far
behind. The simple fact that the Christian life is by its very
essence a corporate life, means that the personal can never
be asserted at the expense of the familial and the local to
the neglect of the broader fellowship.

In many ways the key to sustaining that vision for the
interdependence of Christians and of churches is through
maintaining the focus on the task that we share, namely
the evangelization of the nations. The work Christ left his
followers to do after his ascension was that of going into
all the world and making disciples of all the nations (Matt.
28:19-20). The pursuit of that goal keeps many things in
balance and perspective in the individual and collective
life of God's people. It keeps them ever outward and
upward looking.

Whenever Christians and churches become inward
looking, fragmentation of one sort or another is sure to
follow. It is only as we focus on the world and its need of
the gospel that we are brought face to face with the fact of
our own personal and corporate inadequacy to meet that
need. We are consequently driven to Christ as the One who
not only has commissioned us, but also has promised to
enable us through his Spirit as we pursue that mission in
his name.

To use the language of the book of Hebrews, we will
then 'run with endurance the race that is set before us, fixing
our eyes on Jesus, the author and perfecter of faith' (Heb.
12:1-2). He alone will lift us above our frustrations and
disappointments and encourage us in the fulfilment of his
work for his glory.

Avoiding the Pitfalls

In all of this, the gentle spirit of the dove will be tempered by the astuteness of a serpent. It calls for a love which is truly robust and which in some small way will reflect the love God has for his entire family on earth. The temptation has always been to think that love and truth are incompatible. 'Doctrine divides, love unites' has often been the maxim used to justify the pursuit of relationships which effectively compromise the gospel or quietly condone unchristian behaviour. Such 'love' is not consistent with the pattern of love which is found in Scripture and which is said to be the distinguishing mark of the true community of the faithful (John 13:35). There are indeed pitfalls in the quest for unity which need to be both recognized and avoided.

In the realm of finding resolution for personal conflict, there is no greater snare than that of wrong attitudes. The pursuit of Christ-likeness in conduct is not merely a matter of doing the right thing, but also doing it in the right way. If anything, displaying a right spirit in our dealings with others – especially in conflict situations – is more difficult than simply doing what we know we ought to do. Many disagreements have been exacerbated simply because of an uncharitable or ungracious spirit in an exchange. To show grace and patience towards those who show neither in return is a true test of our conformity to the One whose conduct was so striking for that very reason.

The same is true in the wider vein. On the one hand we need to guard against a spirit of suspicion and even outright cynicism towards those who are not from our circles, while on the other hand we need to seek the widest possible fellowship within the boundaries of gospel truth, always being ready to 'test the spirits to see whether they are from God' (1 John 4:1).

Even though at times the pursuit of these goals within the church and between different churches will seem to be like walking a tightrope, we will make full use of the safety equipment God, in his infinite love and wisdom, has made available.

Soli Deo Gloria

The overriding impetus to persevere in this fraught venture will be the desire for God's glory. As we take the great High Priestly prayer of Christ upon our hearts and also upon our own lips, our longing, like his, will be that there will be a oneness among the people of God that the world will see and will cause them to recognize that Jesus is indeed from God and his gospel message is indisputably true.

No matter how great the fragmentation within churches and between churches, and no matter how discouraged we may be, our confidence is in the promise of Christ that he will ultimately build his church and the gates of hell will not prevail against it (Matt. 16:18). The worst failures of the people of God as individuals and as a body are never beyond the reach of the restoring grace of their Saviour God. The dream of evangelical unity – the unity of those who share the joy of redeeming grace – may well seem elusive in this world. But there is no greater joy than proving in a fallen and fragmented world that there is grace in Jesus Christ that will heal and restore what sin has tried to sunder. That is the gospel!

Notes

[1] *The Westminster Confession of Faith*, 25:5.

[2] *Evangelicals and Catholics Together* is a movement, largely centred in America and the United Kingdom, promoting dialogue between Roman Catholics and Protestants on the basis of shared evangelical beliefs. Its profile has been raised significantly in conservative Protestant circles by the controversy caused by Dr J. I. Packer's involvement in the ongoing discussions.

[3] *The Cambridge Declaration* was issued as the outcome of an historic meeting of 120 evangelical pastors, teachers and leaders of parachurch organizations that took place in Cambridge, Massachusetts, 17–20 April 1996. It was designed to call the evangelical church in America to repent of its worldliness and to seek to recover the biblical, apostolic doctrine that can empower the church and provide integrity for its witness.

[4] The *Alliance of Confessing Evangelicals* was formed in 1994 and is comprised of evangelical pastors, teachers and leaders of parachurch organizations. Its goal is the recovery of the biblical, apostolic witness by the evangelical movement.

[5] *The Westminster Confession of Faith*, 26.1.

[6] See page 31.

[7] Grudem first advanced his views in *The Gift of Prophecy in 1 Corinthians* ((Lanham, MD; UoA Press) 1982.

[8] The identity of 'the Servant of the Lord' in Isaiah is seen ultimately in Christ, but cannot be divorced from Israel as the Lord's servant with a mission to the world in which she failed.

[9] As, for example, 'You will know them by their fruits ...' (Matt. 7:16).

[10] *New International Version*.

SCRIPTURE INDEX

Index of Subjects

Christian Focus Publications publishes biblically-accurate books for adults and children. The books in the adult range are published in three imprints.

Christian Heritage contains classic writings from the past.

Christian Focus contains popular works including biographies, commentaries, doctrine, and Christian living.

Mentor focuses on books written at a level suitable for Bible College and seminary students, pastors, and others; the imprint includes commentaries, doctrinal studies, examination of current issues, and church history.

For a free catalogue of all our titles, please write to
Christian Focus Publications,
Geanies House, Fearn,
Ross-shire, IV20 1TW, Great Britain

For details of our titles visit us on our web site
http://www.christianfocus.com

Christian Focus titles
by
Donald Macleod

A Faith to Live By

In this book the author examines the doctrines detailed in the Westminster Confession of Faith and applies them to the contemporary situation facing the church.

ISBN 1 85792 428 2   *Hardback*   *320 pages*

Behold Your God

A major work on the doctrine of God, covering his power, anger, righteousness, name and being. This book will educate and stimulate deeper thinking and worship.

ISBN 1 876 676 509   *paperback*   256 pages

Rome and Canterbury

This book assesses the attempts for unity between the Anglican and Roman Catholic churches, examining the argument of history, the place of Scripture, and the obstacle of the ordination of women.

ISBN 0 906 731 887   *paperback*   *64 pages*

The Spirit of Promise

This book gives advice on discovering our spiritual role in the local church, the Spirit's work in guidance, and discusses various interpretations of the baptism of the Spirit.

ISBN 0 906 731 448   *paperback*   *112 pages*

Shared Life

The author examines what the Bible teaches concerning the Trinity, then explores various historical and theological interpretations regarding the Trinity, before indicating where some of the modern cults err in their views of the Trinity.

ISBN 1-85792-128-3   *paperback*   *128 pages*

Focus on the Bible Commentaries

Exodus – John L. Mackay*
Deuteronomy – Alan Harman
Judges and Ruth – Stephen Dray
1 Samuel – Ralph Davis
2 Samuel – Ralph Davis
1 and 2 Kings – Robert Fyall*
Proverbs – Eric Lane*
Song of Solomon – Richard Brooks
Isaiah – Paul House
Jeremiah – George Martin
Daniel – Robert Fyall
Hosea – Michael Eaton
Amos – O Palmer Robertson*
Jonah-Zephaniah – John L. Mackay
Haggai-Malachi – John L. Mackay
Matthew – Charles Price (1998)
Mark – Geoffrey Grogan
John – Robert Peterson
1 Corinthians – Paul Barnett
2 Corinthians – Geoffrey Grogan
Galatians – Joseph Pipa*
Ephesians – R. C. Sproul
Philippians – Hywel Jones
1 and 2 Thessalonians – Richard Mayhue
The Pastoral Epistles – Douglas Milne
Hebrews – Walter Riggans (1998)
James – Derek Prime
1 Peter – Derek Cleave
2 Peter – Paul Gardner (1998)
Jude – Paul Gardner
Revelation – Paul Gardner*
Journey Through the Old Testament – Bill Cotton
How To Interpret the Bible – Richard Mayhue

Those marked with an * are currently being written.

60 Great Founders
Geoffrey Hanks

ISBN 1 85792 1402   *large format*   *496 pages*
This book details the Christian origins of 60 organizations, most of which are still committed to the God-given, world-changing vision with which they began. Among them are several mission organizations.

70 Great Christians
Geoffrey Hanks

ISBN 1 871 676 800   *large format*   *352 pages*
The author surveys the growth of Christianity throughout the world through the lives of prominent individuals who were dedicated to spreading the faith. Two sections of his book are concerned with mission; one section looks at the nineteenth century missionary movement, and the other details mission growth throughout the twentieth century.

Mission of Discovery
ISBN 1 85792 2581   *large format*   *448 pages*

The fascinating journal of Robert Murray McCheyne's and Andrew Bonar's journeys throughout Palestine and Europe in the 1840s to investigate if the Church of Scotland should set up a mission to evangelise the Jewish people. From their investigation, much modern Jewish evangelism has developed.

MENTOR TITLES

Creation and Change – Douglas Kelly

A scholarly defence of the literal seven-day account of the creation of all things as detailed in Genesis 1. The author is Professor of Systematic Theology in Reformed Theological Seminary in Charlotte, North Carolina, USA.

large format   ISBN 1 857 92283 2   *272 pages*

The Healing Promise – Richard Mayhue

A clear biblical examination of the claims of Health and Wealth preachers. The author is Dean of The Master's Seminary, Los Angeles, California.

large format   ISBN 1 857 923 002   *288 pages*

Creeds, Councils and Christ – Gerald Bray

The author, who teaches at Samford University, Birmingham, Alabama, explains the historical circumstances and doctrinal differences that caused the early church to frame its creeds. He argues that a proper appreciation of the creeds will help the confused church of today.

large format   ISBN 1 857 92 280 8   *224 pages*

Calvin and the Atonement – Robert Peterson

In this revised and enlarged edition of his book, the author examines several aspects of Calvin's thought on the atonement of Christ seen through the images of Christ as Prophet, Priest, King, Second Adam, Victor, Legal Substitute, Sacrifice Merit, and Example. The author is on the faculty of Covenant Seminary in St. Louis.

large format   ISBN 1 857 923 77 4   *176 pages*

Calvin and the Sabbath – Richard Gaffin

Richard Gaffin of Westminster Theological Seminary in Philadelphia first explores Calvin's comments on the Sabbath in his commentaries and other writings. He then considers whether or not Calvin's viewpoints are consistent with what the biblical writers teach about the Sabbath.

large format   ISBN 1 857 923 76 6   *176 pages*

Also by Mark Johnston
for Christian Focus

Child of a King

A study of the doctrine of adoption

The highest spiritual blessing God gives is to make
believers in Jesus his children. Adoption into the family of
God is a greater privilege than becoming right with God
through receiving forgiveness of one's sins. As his children,
Christians have been given a place of high status and are
entitled to all the benefits that come through this permanent
relationship with their heavenly Father.

Mark Johnson examines different aspects of being 'the child
of a King' and discovers the blessings given to every
believer. He also considers possible errors of understanding,
including whether or not God is the father of all humans
by creation.

B format   ISBN 1857921887   192 pages

Mark Johnston has been minister of Grove Chapel, London since 1994. Prior to that, he was pastor of the Evangelical Presbyterian Church in Richhill in Northern Ireland. His theological studies included several years at Westminster Theological Seminary in Philadelpia, USA. Mark is married with two children. His interests include fishing and photography. His published works include Child of a King (Christian Focus), a study of the doctrine of adoption, contributing several articles to the NIV Thematic Bible (published by Hodder & Stoughton), and a chapter in the book entitled *Gender and Leadership* (Day One Publications).